LEARNING FROM TEXTBOOKS
Theory and Practice

LEARNING FROM TEXTBOOKS
Theory and Practice

Edited by
Bruce K. Britton
University of Georgia
Arthur Woodward
University of Rochester
Marilyn Binkley
U. S. Department of Education

LEA LAWRENCE ERLBAUM ASSOCIATES, PUBLISHERS
1993 Hillsdale, New Jersey   Hove and London

Lawrence Erlbaum Associates, Inc., Publishers
365 Broadway
Hillsdale, New Jersey 07642

Library of Congress Cataloging-in-Publication Data

Learning from textbooks : theory and practice / edited by Bruce K.
   Britton, Arthur Woodward, Marilyn Binkley.
      p. cm.
   Includes bibliographical references (p.   ) and indexes.
   ISBN 0-8058-0677-6
   1. Textbooks—United States. 2. Textbooks—United States—
Evaluation. I. Britton, Bruce K. II. Woodward, Arthur, 1950–
III. Binkley, Marilyn R.
   LB3047.L43 1992
   371.3′2—dc20   91-38521
                                                            CIP

Books published by Lawrence Erlbaum Associates are printed on acid-free
paper, and their bindings are chosen for strength and durability.

Printed in the United States of America
10 9 8 7 6 5 4 3 2

— ■ — ■—

Contents

Introduction:
Learning from Textbooks

Arthur Woodward
Norman Howard School

The array of instructional materials available to elementary and secondary schools is amazing and breathtaking. Laser disks now bring alive in text, sound, and motion the entire contents of an encyclopedia. Microcomputers are available for word processing and the use of a variety of software programs ranging from simulations to drill and practice. Networks make it easy to pass information, programs, and projects from one computer to another. Calculators are inexpensive and support a process and problem-solving approach to mathematics. VCRs are common and allow the flexible use of classroom, home, or commercially produced videotapes. And then, of course, there are the tried and true overheads and filmstrips.

As we might infer from the list just given, advances in instructional technology have made teaching and learning qualitatively different from just a few years ago—or has it? Although the "electronic classroom" is an exciting and transforming vision, not much seems to have changed in the way teachers teach and students learn. In a system that is deeply conservative and highly resistant to change, it is not surprising that the classroom of *our* youth is very similar to the classrooms of our children and grandchildren. Indeed, although much has been said about the "microcomputer revolution" recent reports suggest that the revolution has passed schools by, leaving things only a little different than they were before (see Cuban, 1986; Mathinos & Woodward, 1988).

This is not to say that innovation cannot occur is schools. But, generally speaking, the wonderful potential of electronic media for changing classroom practice remains a potential to which school superintendents, journals and magazines for administrators, school board members, and teachers give much lip service.

Despite the promise of other media, it is quite clear that the print media, especially textbooks, still dominate the classroom. Although there is some disagreement regarding how much teachers use and depend on textbooks (see Woodward & Elliot, 1990), it is clear that textbooks are a ubiquitous part of classroom life. Studies dealing with teacher use of textbooks have used terms such as *rely, depend, closely follow, use,* and so forth without necessarily defining these terms. Clearly, teachers may differ in the degree to which they rely on textbooks. Certainly, neophyte teachers will tend to rely on textbooks more than experienced teachers. In the 1970s and 1980s evidence suggested that many teachers were expected to very closely follow the basal readers and the lesson plans found in the teachers' guides. However, experienced subject matter teachers may use a textbook as a resource or a general outline. Thus, although the degree of dependence on textbooks varies from area to area, teacher to teacher, and from one subject and grade to another, there is not much doubt that textbooks are a feature, and often a very important one, of instruction.

Given the centrality of textbooks to teaching and learning in elementary and secondary schools it is surprising that there is so little research on textbooks. A review of research on textbooks between the 1930s and 1970s (see Woodward, Elliot, & Nagel, 1988) found brief flurries of interest that quickly subsided. In 1983, the publication of *A Nation At Risk* by the National Commission on Excellence and Education appeared to heighten interest in textbook issues and some notable research, some of it reflected in this volume, was stimulated.

Interestingly, textbooks have now become a focus of much political and cultural controversy. The movement advocating a multicultural curriculum has sparked vigorous protests against some textbooks, notably the recently published Houghton Mifflin elementary school social studies series adopted by California. Although there may be a number of inaccuracies or omissions in textbooks that prompt some disquiet, it is not the textbooks themselves that are the real issue. Rather, as in the Kanawha County case and the concerns for the inclusion of women and minorities in the 1970s, textbooks become proxies for dissatisfaction with schools and the polity.

In the debate surrounding textbooks and multiculturalism, research is surprisingly absent. Thus, questions of legitimate knowledge, the role of textbooks, textbook design, policy issues regarding selection, economic issues concerning the marketplace, and the like, are not part of the current debate. Indeed, without the insights of research on considerate text, mentioning, illustrations, and so forth, the current controversy will result in publishers responding to demands for more content not less, and so textbooks will become compendia of bits and pieces of information that on the surface satisfy everyone. The instructional consequences of *not* using our research knowledge about textbooks are quite clear.

In this volume we see how research on important issues on textbook design can advance our knowledge about what makes textbooks effective learning tools and thus inform policymakers, publishers, and those involved in textbook selection. The idea for this book came out of two symposia organized by Marilyn Binkley (U.S. Department of Education) and Arthur Woodward (then at the University of Rochester) at the 1988 annual meeting of the American Educational Research Association. Researchers representing both pure and applied approaches, presented papers on the quality of writing, the role of questions, the role of pictures and illustrations, and the role of auxiliary materials in the design of effective textbooks. At these symposia we saw how research knowledge could inform the design and quality of textbooks. Indeed, the many publishers who attended the meetings could for the first time see the possibility of a bridge between research and practice.

So succesful were the symposia that after some delay Bruce Britton (University of Georgia) and Arthur Woodward (Norman Howard School, Rochester, New York) were able to assemble updated and expanded versions of some of the papers presented at the symposia. Not only do we see these chapters as providing insight into research and its application to textbook design and improvement, but also we hope they stimulate others to follow this lead.

REFERENCES

Cuban, L. (1986) *Teachers and machines: The classroom use of technology since 1920.* New York: Teachers College Press.

Mathinos, D. L., & Woodward, A. (1988). Instructional computing in an elementary school: The rhetoric and reality of an innovation. *Journal of Curriculum Studies, 20*(5), 465–473.

Woodward, A. & Elliot, D. L. (1990). Textbook use and teacher professionalism. In D. L. Elliot & A. Woodward (Eds.), *Textbooks and schooling in the United States* (89th Yearbook of the National Society for the Study of Education). Chicago IL: National Society for the Study of Education.

Woodward, A., Elliot, D. L., & Nagel, K. (1988). *Textbooks in school and society: An annotated bibliography and guide to research.* New York: Garland.

▬ 1 ▬

Impact of Good and Poor Writing on Learners: Research and Theory

Bruce K. Britton
Sami Gulgoz
Shawn Glynn
University of Georgia

Our topic is the quality of writing in textbooks and its impact on learning. The chapter is divided into four sections. The first and second sections review the evidence for two empirically based conclusions about the impact of text quality on learning; the third describes how a theory of learning from text can be applied to rewriting text; and the fourth projects future practice and research in text quality. Our findings and conclusions are as follows:

1. Rewriting existing textbooks can result in improved learning.
2. Judges can accurately select texts from which students will learn the most.
3. We illustrate how Kintsch's theory of reading (Kintsch & van Dijk, 1978) can be applied to rewriting text in order to improve learning.
4. We describe implications of this research and theory for textbook selectors, publishers, and researchers.

1

QUALITY OF WRITING AND LEARNING:
THE EMPIRICAL EVIDENCE

We found 62 empirical studies that investigated the learning of modified texts. This was based on a computerized search of the major education and psychology databases, supplemented in some cases by our own records. The search ended in early 1989. To be included, studies had to compare two or more versions of texts, and report quantitative, empirical measures of learning.

Thirty-Four Successful Attempts to Improve Learning by Rewriting Texts

By "rewriting" we mean *changing* a text, as distinct from just adding to a text. For "changing," we have in mind the sort of thing that authors and editors do when they rewrite successive drafts of a text to improve its quality. The best evidence we have found that rewriting improves learning from textbooks comes from experimental studies in which researchers tried to improve learning by rewriting textbooks and succeeded. We found 18 studies that fit two criteria: (a) Textbook materials were rewritten, and (b) The original textbook material was then tested *against* the rewritten version. The results are shown in Table 1.1. Of the 18 studies, 16 succeeded in significantly improving learning from the texts. The rewriting techniques included (a) reorganization of the order of ideas, (b) signaling the structure of the content, (c) incorporating preview sentences, (d) adding logical connectives and other structural information, (e) changing or removing details, and (f) explicitly stating main ideas and examples. Usually various combinations of these techniques were used, along with less easily specifiable revisions. The subjects of the experiments included students from Grades 3,4,5,6,9,10,12, college students, and adults at work; the tests of learning included free recall, short answer, multiple choice, and problem solving; the tests were given at delays ranging from a few seconds to 1 day, 1 week, and 12 months. The students read school textbooks or training materials on physics, biology, English, linguistics, geography, computer

TABLE 1.1
Box Scores for Rewriting Texts and Judging Learnable Texts

Rewriting Text to Improve Learning		
	Successes	*Failures*
Studies of Textbooks	16	2
Studies of Other		
Natural Documents	4	1
Constructed Texts	14	1

Adding Elements to Text to Improve Learning		
	Successes	*Failures*
Studies of Textbooks	10	2
Studies of Other		
Natural Documents	6	0
Constructed Texts	6	0

Judgments of Text Learnability	
Pairs of Texts for Which College Students Can Select Accurately Which of the Texts Will Be *Learned Better*	Pairs of Texts for Which College Students Cannot Select *Accurately*
19	1

programming, history, army job tasks, or stories from basal readers.[1]

An additional 20 studies were on rewriting nontextbook materials. Five of these used naturally occurring texts that were not textbooks, including texts from trade books on history, philosophy, and science, an insurance policy, an explanation of workers' compensation from an employee handbook, persuasive essays, and a fairy tale. The results showed that rewriting improved learning in four of the five studies.[2]

The rest of the evidence from nontextbook material comes

---

[1]Baumann, 1986; Beck, McKeown, Omanson, & Pople, 1984; Brennan, Bridge, & Winograd, 1988; Britton, Van Dusen, Gulgoz, & Glynn, 1989, Experiments 1 and 3; Britton & Gulgoz, in press; Britton & Radford, 1988; Duffy et al., 1989; Gulgoz, 1989; Hidi & Baird, 1988; Loman & Meyer, 1983; Marshall & Glock, 1978, 1979; Pepper, 1981; Phifer, McNickle, Ronning, & Glover, 1983; Reder & Anderson, 1980; Slater, 1985; Tenenbaum, 1977.

[2]Britton et al., 1989, Experiment 2; Schwarz & Flammer, 1981; Swaney, Janik, Bond, & Hayes, 1981; Tidwell, 1989.

from 15 studies of artificially constructed texts, that is, texts
that did not occur naturally but instead were constructed by
an experimenter in two or more versions. Most experimenters constructed their texts in order to control some
specific variable so they could test its effect on learning. The
results of 14 of the 15 studies showed reliable effects of the
manipulated variables on learning. However, because the
materials did not come from naturally occurring texts, they
may not be representative of textbook materials. On the other
hand, these studies do provide evidence that rewriters can
control some of the variable features of writing that have an
impact on learning.[3]

The Four Failures to Improve Learning by
Rewriting Texts, and
a Recently Resolved Contradiction

In two studies of rewritten textbook materials (Freebody &
Anderson, 1983; Slater, Graves, & Piche, 1985), no reliable
effects on learning were found. Failures to improve learning
were also found in one study of nontextbook materials (Roen
& Piche, 1984) and one study of constructed texts (Slater,
Palmer, & Graves, 1982). In all of these studies, variables
other than rewriting were found to influence learning reliably, providing some indication that the tests of learning may
have been sufficiently sensitive to detect effects of rewriting if
any had been present. These failures provide evidence that
rewriting is not always successful.

In addition, there is some inconsistency within those
studies that found overall positive results. When the data for
individual passages are reported, it sometimes appears that,
whereas some of the passages were substantially improved,
others were not. Table 1.2 shows two such data sets as
examples (from Britton, Van Dusen, Gulgoz, & Glynn, 1989;
Experiments 1 & 2). The most improved texts are listed at the

---

[3]Brandt, 1979; Dooling & Lachman, 1971; Fass & Schumacher, 1978;
Fishman, 1978; Keenan, Baillet, & Brown, 1984; Kieras, 1978; Kintsch &
Yarborough, 1982; Lorch & Lorch, 1985; Mayer, 1983; Meyer, Brandt, &
Bluth, 1980; Meyer & Freedle, 1984; Mohr, Glover, & Ronning 1984; Reder &
Anderson, 1982; Williams, Taylor, & Granger, 1981; Zabrucky, 1986.

TABLE 1.2

Retention Means for Individual Original and Rewritten Texts in Two
Experiments*

Text topics	Percent Retained from Original Version	Percent Retained from Rewritten Version	Retention Difference
	Retention		
	Experiment 1		
M	47	59	12
Nuclear Weapons	33	55	22
Tank Crew Duties	43	63	20
Firing at a Sniper	57	77	20
Controlling Shock	60	77	17
Foot Patrols by MPs	49	64	15
Blasting Caps	29	41	12
Placing Radio Antennas	61	73	12
Duties of Rifle Squad Leaders	32	35	3
Using Radar to Check Vehicle Speeds	43	44	1
Care of the Feet	61	61	0
	Experiment 2		
M	27	32	5
History of a century	27	45	18
Medieval view of science	17	34	17
Liberty	13	29	16
Arms control	32	43	11
Future of humankind	9	17	8
Weights of stars	31	37	6
Running down of the universe	24	29	5
Struggles for existence	41	40	− 1
Archeological report of Wooley	34	33	− 1
Effects of steam power	39	36	− 3
Whitehead's view of physical nature and living nature	23	19	− 4
Scientific analysis	38	27	− 11

*Britton et al. (1989).

top; for the texts near the bottom, there is no apparent recall advantage for the rewritten texts. Because few studies report results separately for each passage, we do not know how widespread this is. These findings provide further evidence that rewriting is not always successful.

There was one recently resolved active controversy over whether a particular kind of rewriting improved texts. Graves and Slater (1986), and Graves et al. (1988) reported that two history texts were improved by each of three sets of rewriters: Time-Life writers, discourse researchers, and college composition teachers. However, Britton et al. (1989, Experiment 3) and Duffy et al. (1989) found in studies of the same texts that only the college composition instructors reliably improved the texts. As Graves and Slater (1991) and Graves et al. (1990) reported, when they replicated their study with improved methodology they found the Britton et al. (1989) and Duffy et al. (1989) results (Britton, Van Dusen, & Gulgoz, 1991), so the controversy has now been resolved in favor of the college composition instructors' revisions.

Five Studies Showing That Rewriting Improved Problem Solving But Not Recall

Interestingly, five studies have shown that some changes in texts can produce effects in opposed directions on different measures of learning. In these studies, the treatment variable caused significant decreases or no change in verbatim recall from the texts, but significantly increased performance on problem solving or inference tests that used the information from the texts.[4] If problem-solving and inference-making performance is the criterion for successful learning, then these studies should be classified as successful. It is interesting that in these studies, the text revision seems to have made verbatim recall worse. That is, the text changes that improved problem solving or inference-making actually made the text less successful by other criteria. Obviously, these studies may represent an important new direction in this research.

---

[4]Caplan & Schooler, 1989; Kintsch, 1990; McDonald, 1987; Mannes & Kintsch, 1987; Mayer, Cook, & Dyck, 1984.

The Use of Readability Formula Variables to Improve Learning

In the early days of textbook rewriting research, it was hoped that learning could be increased by simply using more common words and less complex sentences, as suggested by a naive interpretation of readability formula research. But such rewriting turned out to be of very limited value, as Duffy and Kabance (1982) illustrated. Klare (1963) reviewed the six early studies that varied word or sentence difficulty in a controlled way, and found that only one had a positive effect on learning. Later controlled studies by Coleman (1962), Kniffen et al. (1979), and McCracken (1959) did not find reliable effects on learning either, whereas very small effects were found by Duffy and Kabance (1982), and Siegel, Lambert, and Burkett (1974).

Adding Elements to Texts: Twenty-Two Successful Attempts to Improve Learning

Texts can also be improved by adding linguistic or paralinguistic elements to them without rewriting or otherwise changing the texts. Elements used in this way included headings, logical connectives, preview sentences, underlining, summaries, numbering of listings, and typographical emphasizers such as capitalization, italics, type size, and typeface (Lorch, in press). School textbook materials were modified by adding such elements in 12 studies; 10 succeeded in improving learning and 2 did not. The successful studies included students from Grade 5 through Grade 9, college students, and adults at work. Tests included free recall, multiple choice, and short answer, and the tests were given at delays ranging from immediate to 1 hour, 24 hours, 5 days, 1 week, and 2 weeks. The students read school textbooks or training materials on psychology, history, aircraft mechanics, biology, sociology, earth science, or government, and stories.[5]

---

[5]Brooks, Dansereau, Spurlin, & Holley, 1983; Doctorow, Wittrock, & Marks, 1978; Foster, 1979; Hartley, Kenely, Owen, & Trueman, 1980; Hartley & Trueman, 1985; Hershberger & Terry, 1965; Holley et al., 1981; Klare, Mabry, & Gustafson, 1955; Shebilske & Rotondo, 1981; Wilhite, 1986.

Another source of evidence comes from 6 studies, all successful, in which naturally occurring nontextbook materials were modified by adding elements.[6] Finally, there are 6 successful studies in which artificially constructed texts were modified in this way.[7]

The Two Failures to Improve Learning by Adding Elements to the Texts

Christensen and Stordahl (1955) and Hershberger (1964) did not succeed in improving textbook materials by adding elements, including summaries, underlining, headings, and typographical cuing. However, only Hershberger found reliable effects of other variables on learning, indicating tests sufficiently sensitive to detect effects of rewriting.

QUALITY OF WRITING AND JUDGMENTS OF LEARNABILITY: AN EXPERIMENT WITH 20 TEXTS

The studies reviewed here indicate that some texts are more learnable than others. Presumably, this applies to longer texts as well, up to the length of the textbooks used in schools. Teachers and principals have always been concerned about how learnable textbooks are. We believe their concerns can and should be addressed during the textbook selection process.

Textbook adoption committees want to select textbooks that maximize learnability. Obviously, the committees should consider information about the learnability of the textbooks that are under consideration. However, usually it is impractical for adoption committees to test empirically the learnability of candidate textbooks. But some adoption committees have gone so far as to neglect to consider learnability explicitly at all, using instead such proxies as readability

---

[6]Hartley, Bartlett, & Branthwaite, 1980; Hartley, Goldie, & Steen, 1979; Lorch & Chen, 1986; McLaughlin-Cook, 1981; Spyridakis & Standal, 1986, 1987.

[7]Bransford & Johnson, 1972; Dooling & Lachman, 1971; Glynn & DiVesta, 1979; Lorch, 1985; Parker, 1962; Schallert, 1976.

formulas and copyright date (Tyson-Bernstein, 1988). Perhaps they lack confidence in their judgments of learnability. This raises the important question of whether people can make accurate judgments about the learnability of textbooks.

One recent influential line of evidence seems to suggest that such judgments are very inaccurate: Glenberg and others seemed to have shown that individuals' judgments of text learnability (i.e., how much one has learned from reading a single text) were inaccurate (Glenberg & Epstein, 1985, 1987; Glenberg, Sanocki, Epstein, & Morris, 1987; Glenberg, Wilkinson, & Epstein, 1982; Maki & Berry, 1987; Schommer & Surber, 1986; Walczyk & Hall, 1989). Superficially, this might lead us to expect that judgments of *relative* normative learnability would be at least as poor; if one can't accurately judge one's own learning of a single text, how can one be expected to judge the relative normative learnability of two alternate versions of a text? But Weaver (1990) recently pointed out methodological problems with some of these studies and the findings now appear questionable.

But, in any case, we thought this was a superficial conclusion from the Glenberg literature. In textbook selection, the judgments can be based on direct comparisons of two alternate textbooks; this substantially enriches the judgment situation. The results of such comparisons between texts had not previously been examined, and we thought they might greatly increase the accuracy of the judgments. We therefore collected judgments of normative learnability for original and rewritten versions of 20 texts, where, for each pair of texts, we knew their true normative learnability from previous experiments. Specifically, we tested how well college students could judge which of a pair of texts would be remembered best on a hypothetical test 24 hours later. College students were chosen as subjects because they were readily available. And because college students are the pool from which most future textbook selectors come, the results have implications for the selection of textbooks in schools (Britton, Gulgoz, Van Dusen, Glynn, & Sharp, 1991).

Method

The pairs of texts we tested included 14 pairs for which we already knew from previous experiments that the rewritten version had been remembered better than the original version 24 hours later, and 6 pairs for which we already knew from previous experiments that the rewritten version had not been remembered better than the original (Britton et al., 1989). We gave each student the two members of a pair, and asked for this judgment: "If you were tested 24 hours from now, which of these texts would you *remember the most* from?" Thirty undergraduates made the judgments for each pair of texts.

Results

Table 1.3 shows the results. The top panel shows the results for the 14 texts for which retention was significantly improved by rewriting; the bottom panel shows the results for the 6 texts for which rewriting had no effect on retention. The last column in the top panel shows the percentage of correct judgments for each text. (For the bottom panel, there was no "correct" judgment of which text would be remembered better, because neither had been remembered better in our studies. The figures there represent the proportion of subjects who selected the rewritten version.) The percentages in the last column were tested individually for each passage, using the test for the significance of a percentage. The critical value for $p < .05$ for 30 subjects is 70%.

Of the 14 improved texts, 13 were judged correctly according to the 70% criterion. Of the 6 unimproved texts, all were correctly judged unimproved. The rewritten text that was not judged correctly was a 1943 document that contained the phrase *colored races;* student's negative affective reactions to this term may have spread to affect their judgments of learnability.

Discussion

Of the 20 comparisons, 19 (95%) were accurate. It appears likely that textbook selection committees could do better than this. For example, they could use this set of text pairs as a pretest to select persons who can judge more accurately than these average college students. Accuracy might be improved further by a modest training program that simply provided feedback to judges about the accuracy of their judgments on this set of text pairs.

TABLE 1.3
Results of Text Judgments Study

Improved Texts

Topic	Source of Original Version	Rewriters	Percent Improvement in Retention Observed from Original to Rewritten Version in Previous Studies	Percent Correct Judgments of Learnability
Tank Crew Duties	Army Training Manual	Kern, Sticht, Welty, & Hauke (1976)	20	83*
Blasting Caps	Army Training Manual	Kern et al. (1976)	12	80*
Snipers	Army Training Manual	Kern et al. (1976)	20	87*
Controlling Shock	Army Training Manual	Kern et al. (1976)	17	77*
Korean War	Textbook	College Composition Instructors	8	73*
Vietnam War	Textbook	College Composition Instructors	10	77*
Korean War	Time-Life Writers	College Composition Instructors	9	70*
Vietnam War	Time-Life Writers	College Composition Instructors	10	73*
Korean War	Discourse Researchers	College Composition Instructors	7	87*
Vietnam War	Discourse Researchers	College Composition Instructors	12	70*
Mitosis	Textbook	Britton and Radford (1988)	16	97*

(continued)

TABLE 1.3 (Continued)

Improved Texts

Topic	Source of Original Version	Rewriters	Percent Improvement in Retention Observed from Original to Rewritten Version in Previous Studies	Percent Correct Judgments of Learnability
History of a Century	Viscount Castlerosse	Graves & Hodge (1943)	18	97*
Medieval View of Science	J.W.N. Sullivan	Graves & Hodge (1943)	17	87*
Liberty	Viscount Samuel	Graves & Hodge (1943)	16	37

Unimproved Texts

Topic	Comparison Version	Revision	Percent Improvement in Retention Observed from Comparison Version to Revision in Britton et al. (1989)	Percent Judgments that Revision was Better
Korean War	Textbook	Time-Life Writers	1	47
Vietnam War	Textbook	Time-Life Writers	0	50
Korean War	Textbook	Discourse Researchers	1	50
Vietnam War	Textbook	Discourse Researchers	2	60
Korean War	Time-Life	Discourse Researchers	2	50
Vietnam War	Time-Life	Discourse Researchers	2	67

*$p < .05$

This result is consistent with a positive assessment of the value of text learnability judgments. The incorporation of accurate learnability judgments into the textbook selection process may have beneficial effects. First, if more learnable textbooks are selected, presumably more learning will occur. Second, once learnability judgments are routinely used by textbook selectors, then the publishers, following the demand of the market, will try to attend more effectively to the learnability of their textbooks. If any publishers succeed in improving the learnability of their textbooks, then selection committees using learnability judgments will presumably detect this and can reward those publishers by selecting their textbooks. In turn, this may encourage the other publishers to try to improve the learnability of their textbooks. We can envision successive cycles of improvement, leading to more high quality textbooks and more learning among students.

A COGNITIVE THEORY OF LEARNING FROM TEXT APPLIED TO REWRITING TEXT TO IMPROVE LEARNING

For several years, Kintsch and his associates have been developing a theory of human learning from text (Kintsch & van Dijk, 1978; Miller & Kintsch, 1980; van Dijk & Kintsch, 1983). Our purpose here is to describe how Kintsch's theory can be applied to rewriting an instructional text to improve learning from the text. From our point of view, Kintsch's theory proposes that learners try to build a mental representation of the information they are trying to learn from the text. They have four sources of help they can call on—two sources coming from the learner, and two sources from the text. The learner provides:

1. His or her prior knowledge about the topics in the text; this we call *declarative prior knowledge;* and
2. His or her mental programs and the habits he or she has acquired for dealing with text and learning; these we call *procedural prior knowledge.*

The text provides:

1. The content elements of the text (the facts and ideas expressed in the phrases and sentences) and
2. What we call *construction instructions,* which are text elements that instruct the learner how to construct his or her representation.

Construction instructions are present in all text. Some construction instructions are expressed in paralinguistic form and some in language. For example, the paragraph boundary is a paralinguistic construction instruction. Conventionally, it tells the learner to finish off one part of his or her representation and start constructing the next part. A heading above the paragraph is a construction instruction that tells the learner what she or he should put at the head of his or her mental representation. Further instructions about the shape of the representation can be provided by the heading's position, color, underlining, typeface, and type size. Many other paralinguistic features can serve as construction instructions. A heading may also provide linguistic instructions for the eventual shape of the to-be-constructed representation, as in the language of a heading like "Three Types of Widgets, with Common, Characteristic, and Differentiating Features of Each."

Construction instructions can also be embodied in entirely linguistic form. "For example" tells the learner that the rest of the sentence is to be related by the relation "example-of" to the previous sentence. Other such relations are specified by phrases like "importantly," "secondly," "a discussion of these two strategies follows," "I shall conclude by," "In summary," and so forth. Syntactic features of text can also serve as construction instructions. For example, the fact that a word is the syntactic subject of a sentence can be used as an instruction to give it a privileged status in the construction of the sentence's mental representation (Givon, in press).

So construction instructions are ubiquitous in text. But the learner need not use them. Whether she or he uses them depends on the mental programs and habits she or he has acquired for dealing with text and learning: his or her procedural prior knowledge about how to use text for learning information. The construction instructions and the learner's programs for using them provide the procedural information that the learner needs to take action on the text to construct his or her representation. The construction instructions are like the blueprints for constructing a building, and the learner's reading habits provide the program for implementing those blueprints.

But the building must also be made out of something: Structural members are needed for construction, too.

For texts, these structural members include (a) the content elements of the text, including the facts and ideas expressed in it; and (b) the reader's prior knowledge about those facts and ideas.

Together these four sources of help are used by the learner to construct his or her mental representation of the text. The way the sources of help are used differs from text to text and learner to learner; the general idea can be illustrated best by considering an extended example. Because Kintsch's theories have been largely concerned with the coherence of text, our example will be largely concerned with the learners' efforts to establish coherence relations between the parts of a text so that the parts of the text will be linked to each other. And the rewriting we will implement and test will be directed toward repairing the text so that the learner can more easily establish coherence relations.

An Example of How Kintsch's Theory Can be Used to Improve Text Learnability

Consider Examples 1 and 2, which are the title and the first sentence of a text about Vietnam (Air Force Reserve Officers Training Corps [ROTC], 1985):

1. Title: "Air War in the North, 1965"
2. By the fall of 1964, Americans in both Saigon and Washington had begun to focus on Hanoi as the source of the continuing problem in the South.

The title can be treated as a construction instruction, instructing the learner to place the topic specified in the title at the head of his or her mental representation, and to interpret all the rest of the text in relation to it. This construction instruction will probably be used in this way, even by a learner with only average skills and motivation. Learners with more well-developed mental programs and habits for learning from text may go further—if they are well motivated they may use 1 as an instruction to activate relevant prior knowledge (about war, air war, the North, and 1965), to generate appropriate questions for themselves (e.g., what caused the air war?), or to implement a variety of other thought elaborations that skilled learners use when they are highly motivated.

But not all learners will carry out the construction instructions or even notice them. There are readers with below average skill or motivation for whom 1 will not cue any construction instructions, or, even if it does, they may be so passive as to fail to carry them out.

When 2 is read, most learners will try to relate it back to the title, because we all learn early in life that each part of a connected discourse is linked to at least one other part of it. That is, we try to establish coherence in texts (Halliday & Hasan, 1976; Kintsch & van Dijk, 1978; van Dijk & Kintsch, 1983). We all have mental programs and habits for creating such coherence links. Following the Law of Least Effort (Zipf, 1949), we will probably try to use the easiest program. The easiest program for linking one sentence to another is to look for some idea that is common to the two sentences, and the easiest way to find a common idea is to look for a repetition of the same content word. But in 1 and 2, there is no repetition of a content word. So a linguistic construction instruction that is needed for executing this program is missing from the text.

At this point, the learner faces a choice point, one of a great many she or he will encounter throughout the processing of any text. If the learner is to establish coherence by linking 2 back to 1, she or he must do some extra mental work. If the person fails to do the extra mental work, then the first sentence will not be linked to the title. Suppose the learner chooses not to do the extra mental work: What are the consequences for learning? One clear consequence is that the first sentence will not be accessible in memory from the title because they are not linked. So if the learner is given a test of learning with the title as a cue—a common test situation— she or he will fail to retrieve the information in the first sentence.

Let us consider the learner's other choice: suppose the person does try to link 2 back to 1. The first step will be to activate a relevant mental program. One such program is to activate related prior knowledge and see if some overlap between 2 and 1 can be created in that way. From here the learner can take one of several paths, depending on the content of his or her prior knowledge.

One path would lead the learner to think along these lines: "I know that events in the late part of one year can cause events in the next year, and the fall of 1964 comes just before 1965, so perhaps that is the relation that links 2 back to 1." When she or he thinks that, then the learner can add this prior knowledge to his or her mental representation of the sentence. We can show the mental consequence of this line of thinking by using parentheses to insert the activated prior knowledge into the mental representation of the sentence, as follows:

3. Title: Air War in the North, 1965
4. By the fall of 1964 (causing events in 1965), Americans in both Saigon and Washington had begun to focus on Hanoi as the source of the continuing problem in the South.

Now 2, supplemented as in 4, shares an idea in common with the title—namely 1965—and so the learner can link them to one another. So if 3 is given as a cue in a test, then 4 will be accessible via the idea of the year 1965.

This particular connection is easy to make; it can be established by anyone who has prior knowledge about the causal relation of events in successive years. This sort of general prior knowledge is probably available to any normal adult. The only behavioral sign of creating this linkage may be a brief look back at the 1965 in the title, and even this may be attenuated or replaced by an unobservable look back into the short term memory representation of the title.

There is also another path the learner can follow, because there is an alternative way of linking 2 back to 1. But this path is open only to readers with *both* of two items of domain-specific prior knowledge, specifically that "the North" refers to North Vietnam, *and* that Hanoi is the capitol of North Vietnam. By activating this knowledge and adding it to his/her mental representation, the learner creates this representation:

    5. Title: Air War in the North (Vietnam), 1965
    6. By the fall of 1964, Americans in both Saigon and Washington had begun to focus on Hanoi (capitol of North Vietnam) as the source of the continuing problem in the South.

Now 6 shares in common with 5 the idea of North Vietnam, so a test with 5 as a cue will give access to 6 via the link of North Vietnam.

    There is yet a third path the learner can take: She or he can make both links. If both these links are made, then the learner's representation is:

    7. Title: Air War in North (Vietnam) 1965
    8. By the fall of 1964 (causing events in 1965), Americans in both Saigon and Washington had begun to focus on Hanoi (capitol of North Vietnam) as the source of the continuing problem in the South.

Here the consequence for learning is that the learner can get access to the ideas in 8 from either of two ideas in 7: the idea of 1965 or the idea of North Vietnam. This will further increase the retrievability of the sentence, because if one forgets one retrieval route, one can use the other route instead.

    This two-sentence example, from a text originally chosen more or less at random, contains examples of all the sources of information that the learner uses to construct his representation: From the learner comes his programs and habits for reading and learning and his declarative prior knowledge about things mentioned in the text, and from the text comes the content elements of the sentences and the construction instructions expressed by the title. This text is not unusual; almost any text has examples of all four sources of information.

    Also, many texts have missing information that the learner has to infer (Britton, Van Dusen, Glynn, & Hemphill, 1990) if he or she is to have a coherent text. This example also shows the variety of different paths the learner can choose, from not trying to link 2 back to 1 at all, to linking them in one of two possible ways, or the other, or both. There are four possibilities in all here, each one leading to a different mental representation for the learner, as represented schematically in Fig. 1.1. Each mental representation has different consequences for learning.

How does this relate to the impact of text quality on learning? The criterion differentiating high quality instructional texts from low quality ones is this: High quality texts are written so that readers can easily construct high quality

No Links

Air War in the North, 1965

By the Fall of 1964   Americans in both Saigon and
                                                 Washington had begun to focus
                                                 on Hanoi as the source of the
                                                 problem in the South.

One Link Based on General Prior Knowledge

Air War in the North, 1965

By the Fall of 1964   Americans in both Saigon and
(causing events in 1965)   Washington had begun to focus
                                                 on Hanoi as the source of the
                                                 problem in the South.

One Link Based on Domain-Specific Prior Knowledge

Air War in the North (Vietnam), 1965

By the Fall of 1964   Americans in both Saigon and
                                                 Washington had begun to focus
                                                 on Hanoi (capitol of North Viet-
                                                 nam) as the source of the
                                                 problem in the South.

Both Links

Air War in the North (Vietnam), 1965

By the Fall of 1964   Americans in both Saigon and
(causing events in 1965)   Washington had begun to focus
                                                 on Hanoi (capitol of North Viet-
                                                 nam) as the source of the
                                                 problem in the South.

FIG. 1.1 Four possible ways of linking the title and first sentence of the Example text.

mental representations—ones that are correct, complete, and easily retrievable. Low quality texts produce low quality mental representations—incorrect, incomplete in important ways, or not retrievable.

What happens when we apply this criterion to the example text? Alas, we must conclude that the text in 1 and 2 leaves a great deal to be desired. Only readers who (a) have substantial prior knowledge about the Vietnam War and (b) use it to infer coherence-creating links can hope to connect the parts of the text in a maximally retrievable way.

How might the quality of this text be improved? One way is by rewriting the text to ease the reader's task. This can be done by providing the information that the person needs to relate the different parts of the text, as here:

9. Title: Air War in North Vietnam, 1965
10. By the beginning of 1965, Americans in both Saigon and Washington had begun to focus on Hanoi, capitol of North Vietnam, as the source of the continuing problem in the South.

The main empirical claim presented here is that the quality of a text can be improved by altering the text so the reader can more easily create a correct, complete, and retrievable representation. If the text calls for the reader to do lots of extra mental work to create a good representation, many readers will fail to do the work or do it wrong, and so their representation will be poor. But if the text makes it easy to create a good representation, more readers will do it, and more learning will occur.

This theory of learning from text has several implications that are borne out by empirical studies. First, the theory implies that texts that provide more coherent links will be recalled better than texts with fewer such links. This has been confirmed by a study in which there was a correlation of .80 between the number of links the text included, and the amount of recall. The more coherent links the text provided, the higher the level of recall (Britton, Van Dusen, Glynn, & Hemphill, 1990). Second, the theory implies that texts with explicit construction instructions will be learned better than texts without them. This is confirmed by the studies reviewed earlier of adding explicit construction instructions:

headings, numbering, typographical cues, and so forth. Third, the theory implies that texts will be learned better if the materials needed for establishing coherence are provided so the learner can produce a mental representation that is coherent. This claim is confirmed most clearly by several studies from our laboratory; here we describe a study of learning the same text that we have been using as an example in the last section (Britton & Gulgoz, in press).

AN EXPERIMENT IN REWRITING TEXT TO IMPROVE LEARNING

The original text, from a textbook used in Air Force ROTC (1985), is shown in Table 1.4, and revisions we constructed using our theory are shown in Tables 1.5 and 1.6. We invite further investigations of these texts.

Principled Revision

We began by analyzing the text with Kintsch's computer program (Young, 1984) to detect the locations where coherence relations broke down. Using the principles of Kintsch's program, we refined this analysis to identify the specific problematic links in the coherence of the text. We found 40 problematic links. We then rewrote the text to repair those links.

The version in Table 1.5 is called the Principled Revision because we revised it by applying principles based on Kintsch's theory, including the following:

Principle 1. Make it easier for the learner to establish coherence by rewriting each sentence so that it repeats the linking word from the previous sentence.

We have already illustrated this in 9 and 10. The principle was applied extensively throughout the original text in Table 1.4. For example, in the second sentence (of Table 1.4) the phrase "the inability of the ARVN to defeat the enemy in the field" is actually the same thing as the first sentence's "the continuing problem in the South." That is, "the inability of ARVN to defeat the enemy in the field" simply *is* "the

TABLE 1.4
Original Version of Example Text
Air War in the North, 1965

By the fall of 1964, Americans in both Saigon and Washington had begun to focus on Hanoi as the source of the continuing problem in the South. As frustration mounted over the inability of the ARVN to defeat the enemy in the field, pressure to strike directly at North Vietnam began to build. Although there was near unanimity among American officials over the aerial extension of the war into North Vietnam, serious differences arose over both the objective and the methods to be used.

Most members of the Johnson Administration believed bombing attacks would accomplish several things. They would demonstrate clearly and forcefully the United States' resolve to halt Communist aggression and to support a free Vietnam. At the same time, they would provide a boost for the sagging morale of the South Vietnamese. They would also make Hanoi pay an increasingly high price for supporting the Vietcong. Particularly among civilian advocates, the motivation for such a campaign was psychological rather than military, the primary objective not being Hanoi's capability but its willingness to support the war. "In a very real sense," explained Maxwell Taylor, "the objective of our air campaign is to change the will of the enemy leadership."

Those who stressed the psychological impact favored the strategy of "graduated response," a series of escalating attacks designed to show American resolve at relatively low cost while allowing the North Vietnamese leadership to realize the potential cost of supporting the war and thus cease that support before suffering the consequences. If they did not change their ways, severity of the attacks would gradually be increased, with pauses between each increment to allow the enemy time to come to their senses. According to this theory, it would be the fear of future damage that would convince the enemy to cease their aggression. As late as the summer of 1965, Secretary of Defense Robert McNamara argued, "At any time, 'pressure' on the Democratic Republic of Vietnam (DRV) depends not upon the current level of bombing but rather upon the credible threat of future destruction which can be avoided by agreeing to negotiate. . . ." Graduated response assumed North Vietnam would not risk its fragile and limited industrial base in the face of overwhelming American power and would quickly succumb to the pressure thus exerted.

The Joint Chiefs of Staff (JCS), particularly Air Force Chief of Staff General John P. McConnell, adamantly opposed this approach. Graduated response, they contended, was a weak and indecisive strategy. It would not provide a clear symbol of our determination and resolve because of its incremental nature; nor would it damage Hanoi's war-making capability rapidly enough to be effective. Moreover, gradual escalation would give the enemy time to prepare psychologically and materially for each new step. The military leaders emphasized destruction of the enemy's capability to support the war rather than his will and favored brief but intensive operations to eliminate Hanoi's war-making capacity and to demonstrate the strength of the United States' commitment to win the war in a military sense.

(continued)

22

TABLE 1.4 *(Continued)*

In February 1965, President Johnson approved bombing operations against a selective list of targets in North Vietnam. While the government played down the significance of this step. Operation Rolling Thunder, which actually begin in March, represented an important shift in the American approach to the war. The air raids following the Tonkin Gulf incident had been retaliatory strikes in response to specific attacks on American military forces. Rolling Thunder, in contrast, was linked more broadly to the "larger pattern of aggression" by both the Vietcong and the North Vietnam. Washington was now holding North Vietnam directly responsible for the war in the South.

From the beginning, Rolling Thunder was hedged with restrictions and limitations on sortie rates, targets, and even tactics and bomb loads. Rarely has the use of air power been so strictly controlled by civilians. Target selection, sortie rates, and routes were decided on a weekly (later biweekly) basis by a small group composed of the President, the Secretaries of Defense and State, and a handful of other senior officials only loosely guided by recommendations from CINCPAC and the JCS. Washington imposed restrictions of 30 and 15 nautical miles respectively around the capital city of Hanoi and the port of Haiphong. Intended to reduce the risk of superpower confrontation and to limit civilian casualties, these restrictions immediately limited the effectiveness of the campaign because the two cities were the center of North Vietnam's industrial base and the entry points for supplies from the Soviet Union and the People's Republic of China. Also off-limits was a strip thirty miles wide along the Chinese border.

By summer, Rolling Thunder had grown in intensity. The possible target area had been extended from the 19th parallel to the 20th parallel and then moved still further north. In addition to specified "hard targets" (stationary), strike forces had limited freedom to attack targets of opportunity in certain designated areas. Targets included military barracks, naval bases, railroad yards, ferries, bridges, road repair equipment, and lines of communication (LOCs). The total number of sorties had risen to 900 a week, more than four times that of March.

Yet the bombing campaign had not achieved its objective. American policymakers had conceived of graduated response as a "low cost option with prospects for speedy, positive results." However, Hanoi showed no signs of quitting. In the words of a CIA assessment of the early operations, "The strikes to date have not caused a change in the North Vietnamese policy. . . . If anything, the strikes . . . have hardened their attitude."

The failure to obtain results led to a perceptible shift in the nature of the air war. While Rolling Thunder would continue, by July 1965 the objective slowly shifted from that of attacking psychological targets to the interdiction of North Vietnamese men and materials moving south. Whatever had been the hopes cherished by some officials in February and March, civilian leaders now conceived of the air campaign against the North as complementary to the ground war in the South. Reflecting this shifting objective, greater emphasis was placed on enemy lines of communication both in the panhandle of North Vietnam and along the Ho Chi Minh Trail in eastern Laos.

TABLE 1.5
Principled Revision
The 1965 Air War in North Vietnam

By the beginning of 1965, American officials in both South Vietnam and the United States had begun to focus on North Vietnam as the source of the continuing war in South Vietnam. The South Vietnamese army was losing the ground war against North Vietnam and this caused frustrations among the American officials. The frustrations led to pressure to bomb North Vietnam. The idea of bombing North Vietnam found support among nearly all the American officials. However, the civilian and military officials had serious differences over both the objective and the methods of the bombing attacks.

Most of both civilian and military members of the Johnson administration believed bombing attacks would accomplish several things. The bombing attacks would demonstrate clearly and forcefully the United States' resolve to halt communist North Vietnam's aggression and to support a free South Vietnam. At the same time, the bombing attacks would provide a boost for the South Vietnamese morale, which was sagging because they were losing the war. The bombing attacks would also make North Vietnam pay an increasingly high price for supporting the war. Among the civilian officials, the motivation for the bombing attacks was psychological rather than military. For the civilian officials, the primary objective of the bombing was to break North Vietnam's willingness to support the war rather than its ability. Maxwell Taylor explained the civilian view: "The objective of our air campaign is to change the will of the enemy leadership."

In order to reach their psychological objective, the civilian officials favored the strategy of "graduated response." The graduated response strategy was designed to show at relatively low cost the American resolve to stop North Vietnamese aggression. Graduated response was a series of increasing attacks with pauses after each increase to allow the North Vietnamese leaders to realize the potential cost of supporting the war. When they realized the potential cost, the North Vietnamese leaders would cease supporting the war before suffering the consequences. If the North Vietnamese leaders did not cease supporting the war, the intensity of the bombing attacks would be further increased, with pauses between each attack to allow the North Vietnamese to realize the threat of future increases. According to the graduated response strategy, it would be the threat of future damage that would convince the North Vietnamese to cease their aggression. Secretary of Defense Robert McNamara explained that the pressure of the civilian strategy on North Vietnam "depends not upon the current level of bombing but rather upon the credible threat of future destruction which can be avoided by agreeing to negotiate. . . ." The graduated response strategy assumed that North Vietnamese leaders would not risk the destruction of their fragile and limited industry by overwhelming American power. Therefore, they would quickly give in and cease their aggression.

(continued)

TABLE 1.5 *(Continued)*

The graduated response strategy did not find support among the military officials, particularly Air Force Chief of Staff General John P. McConnell. The military officials believed that the graduated response strategy was a weak and indecisive strategy. They believed the graduated response strategy would not be a clear symbol of U.S. determination and resolve because its intensity increased gradually. They also believed that this strategy would not damage North Vietnam's war-making ability rapidly enough to be effective. They believed that the pauses before each increase would give the North Vietnamese time to prepare psychologically and materially for the next bombing attack. Instead, the military officials thought it was more important to destroy North Vietnam's ability to support the war. In order to destroy North Vietnam's war-making ability and to show the strength of the United States resolve to win the war, the military officials favored brief and intensive bombing attacks.

The graduated response strategy was President Johnson's choice. In February 1965, he approved bombing attacks against a selective list of targets in North Vietnam. The Johnson administration played down the importance of attacking North Vietnam directly. However, these bombing attacks, which began in March under the code name of Rolling Thunder, represented an important shift in the American approach to the war in Vietnam. Before Rolling Thunder, American attacks on North Vietnam, like the air raids following the Tonkin Gulf incident, had been retaliatory attacks in response to specific attacks on American military forces. In contrast to these retaliatory attacks, Rolling Thunder aimed at the "larger patter of aggression" by North Vietnam. By Operation Rolling Thunder, American officials were now holding North Vietnam directly responsible for the war in South Vietnam.

From the beginning, the bombing attacks of Operation Rolling Thunder had many restrictions and limitations. Restrictions included the rates of bombing attacks, targets, and even tactics and bomb loads. Aerial bombing attacks have rarely been so strictly controlled by civilians before. A small civilian group composed of the President, the Secretaries of Defense and State, and a handful of other senior officials made decisions about target selection, attack rates, and routes. The decisions of the civilian officials were only loosely guided by recommendations from military officials. The civilian officials imposed restrictions of 30 nautical miles around the North Vietnamese capital city of Hanoi and 15 nautical miles around the port of Haiphong. Such restrictions were intended to limit civilian casualties and to reduce the risk of confrontation between the United States and the Soviet Union or China. However, these restrictions immediately limited the effectiveness of the bombing attacks because Hanoi and Haiphong were the center of North Vietnam's industry and these cities were also the entry point for supplies from the Soviet Union and People's Republic of China. A restriction with a similar effect was a strip 30 miles wide along the Chinese border.

(continued)

TABLE 1.5 *(Continued)*

The bombing attacks of the graduated response strategy had increased in intensity by the summer of 1965. An example of the increase was that the possible target area had been extended from the 19th parallel to the 20th parallel to cover a larger area in North Vietnam, and then the target area was moved still further North. Also, in addition to targets specified by the civilian officials, bombing forces had limited freedom to attack targets of opportunity in certain areas. Such targets of opportunity included military barracks, naval bases, railroad yards, ferries, bridges, road repair equipment, and lines of communication (LOCs). The total number of attacks had risen to 900 a week, which was four times the number of attacks when Rolling Thunder began. Despite such an increase in the intensity of the attacks, the bombing attacks had not achieved the objective of breaking the will of the North Vietnamese. The civilian officials, who favored graduated response, had conceived of these bombing attacks as a "low cost option with prospects for speedy, positive results." However, the result of the attacks was that North Vietnamese showed no signs of quitting. This was confirmed by a CIA report: "The strikes to date have not caused a change in the North Vietnamese policy. . . . If anything, the strikes . . . have hardened their attitude."

The failure of the graduated response strategy to obtain positive results led to a clear shift in the nature of the air war. The shift was from the civilian strategy of attacking psychological targets to stopping forcefully the North Vietnamese soldiers and materials moving to South Vietnam. When Rolling Thunder began, before the civilian officials shifted to their new view, they had hoped that graduated response strategy would stop the war. Because the war was still going on, the civilian officials shifted to the view that the objective of the aerial bombing attacks against North Vietnam was to help win the ground war in South Vietnam. Reflecting this shift in the civilian view, greater emphasis was placed on bombing North Vietnam's lines of communication both in the panhandle of North Vietnam and along the Ho Chi Minh Trail in eastern Laos.

continuing problem in the South." But many learners will miss this connection, because no content words are repeated across the two sentences. In the Principled Revision, we changed the first sentence to read "the continuing *war* in South Vietnam" and the second sentence to read "the South Vietnamese army was losing the ground *war* against North Vietnam." We expected that some of the learners who would otherwise have missed it would see the link and incorporate it in their representation, creating a more correct and complete representation and establishing additional ·retrieval routes for themselves.

We also made some additional changes in those phrases. These changes were motivated by a corrolary of Principle 1.

TABLE 1.6
Heuristic Revision
Air War in North Vietnam, 1965

By January 1965, President Johnson had concluded that North Vietnam was winning the war against South Vietnam. To prevent Vietnam from winning the war, the President's advisers decided that the United States should bomb North Vietnam. They believed that the bombing of North Vietnam would accomplish three things:

1. The bombing attacks would damage parts of North Vietnam, causing the North Vietnamese to realize that it was costly for them to continue the war.
2. The bombing attacks would convince North Vietnam that the United States was determined to stop them from conquering South Vietnam.
3. The bombing would also convince South Vietnam's army that the United States was determined to stop North Vietnam, and this would improve morale among the South Vietnamese troops, which was low because they were losing the war.

However, there were serious disagreements about the bombing attacks between President Johnson's civilian advisers and his military advisers. They disagreed on two things: (a) the objective of the bombing attacks, and (b) the method to be used.

The civilian advisers thought that the objective of the bombing campaign should be a psychological objective, namely "to break the will" of the North Vietnamese leadership. One important civilian adviser, Maxwell Taylor, said: "the objective of our air campaign is to change the will of the enemy leadership."

Regarding the method of the bombing attacks, the civilian advisers recommended the strategy of "graduated response." In the graduated response strategy, the United States would launch bombing attacks; at first, small ones that would threaten to damage North Vietnam's industries, which were tiny and fragile. The graduated response strategy would be applied in several steps:

1. First, the United States would launch a few small bombing attacks.
2. Then, the United States would pause to allow the North Vietnamese leadership to see how much damage had been done to their industries.
3. When the North Vietnamese saw how much damage had been done, they would conclude:
   a. that American air power was overwhelming, and
   b. that North Vietnam's industries could be completely destroyed if the U.S. continued the bombing attacks.
4. This would "break the will" of the North Vietnamese, and they would stop making war against South Vietnam.
5. But if the North Vietnamese will had not been broken, the United States would launch bigger bombing attacks, again followed by a pause, and the sequence would be repeated, until North Vietnam gave in.

(continued)

27

TABLE 1.6 *(Continued)*

As one civilian adviser, Secretary of Defense Robert McNamara, said, "U.S. pressure on North Vietnam . . . depends not upon the current level of bombing but rather upon the credible threat of future destruction, which can be avoided by agreeing to negotiate . . ."

In summary, the graduated response strategy assumed North Vietnam would not risk the future destruction of its small, fragile industries, and the will of the North Vietnamese leadership would quickly be broken by their fear of the overwhelming American bombing attacks.

President Johnson's military advisers favored a different strategy. The military advisers (the Joint Chiefs of Staff) thought that the objective of the bombing attacks should be to destroy the industries and military forces of North Vietnam. Once its industries and military power were sufficiently destroyed, North Vietnam would no longer be able to make war on South Vietnam. The military advisers thought that the method of the bombing attacks should be to launch very large bombing attacks that would damage North Vietnam quickly. In summary, the military's strategy was to bomb North Vietnam's industries and military forces briefly, but heavily, and cause enough destruction to force North Vietnam to give up their war on South Vietnam.

In February 1965, President Johnson approved the decision to bomb North Vietnam. The bombing attacks were code named "Operation Rolling Thunder." Johnson's civilian and military advisers agreed that Operation Rolling Thunder was an important change in United States policy. Before Rolling Thunder, the United States had not held North Vietnam responsible for the war. But the bombing attacks of Rolling Thunder served notice on North Vietnam that they were being held responsible for their war on South Vietnam.

For Rolling Thunder, President Johnson chose the graduated response strategy of his civilian advisers instead of the military advisers' strategy. The President met weekly with his civilian advisers (the Secretaries of State and Defense, and a few other senior officials) to make the major decisions about:

—the size of the bombing attacks.
—which targets to bomb.
—routes the aircraft would take to the targets.

Following the graduated response strategy, the first bombing attacks were small (about 200 aircraft each week), and no bombing was allowed in large areas of North Vietnam, including:

—most of the Northern part of North Vietnam.
—the capital city of North Vietnam (Hanoi) and a circle 30 miles around it.
—the main seaport of North Vietnam (Haiphong) and a circle 15 miles around it.
—along the Chinese border, on a strip 30 miles wide.

(continued)

TABLE 1.6 (Continued)

The purpose of not bombing in these areas was to limit civilian casualties and to prevent confrontations between the United States and Russia, or China, who all had many ships delivering war material into Haiphong.

Following the graduated response strategy, the first small bombing attacks of Rolling Thunder were followed by a pause. But North Vietnam did not give in. In a report to President Johnson, the CIA said: "The strikes to date have not caused a change in the North Vietnamese policy. . . . If anything, the strikes . . . have hardened their attitude."

Therefore, still following the graduated response strategy, further rounds of bombing attacks were launched. By June 1965, the bombing attacks were:

—much larger in size (more than 900 per week and more than 4 times as many as in the beginning).
—over a much larger area, including most of North Vietnam.
—against many more targets; and pilots who happened to spot targets could bomb them, including: military barracks, naval bases, railroad yards, ferries, bridges, road repair equipment, and lines of communication.

But the bombing attacks still did not cause North Vietnam to give in. The graduated response strategy had failed.

The failure of the graduated response strategy led to a change in United States bombing policy. In July 1965, the bombing attacks were redirected against North Vietnamese soldiers and materials moving toward South Vietnam, and against their lines of communication in North Vietnam and Laos.

This corrolary was applied when we found that the Original Version used many different terms for the same concept:

Twelve different terms for bombing attacks (e.g., *air war, strike directly, aerial extension, bombing attacks, campaign, air campaign, attacks, bombing, American power, bombing operations, air raids, air power*); 23 different terms for American officials; 15 different terms for North Vietnam; 6 different terms for South Vietnam.

So we applied Principle 1 to change these to the same terms whenever possible. In the first and second sentences, this motivated the change from "Americans" in the Original to "American officials," in the Principled Revision; also "Saigon" to "South Vietnam"; "South" to "South Vietnam"; and "ARVN" to "South Vietnamese Army."

Principle 2. Make coherence easier to establish by arranging the parts of each sentence so the learner *first* encounters the part of the sentence that specifies *where* that sentence is to be connected to the rest of the mental representation; and *second,* encounters the other part of the sentence, which tells the learner *what* new information to add to the previously specified location in the mental representation.

We can do this because nearly every sentence has an "old" part—sometimes called the "given" part—(by which it is connected to the previous text), and a "new" part, which adds the new information by which the text's representation grows (Haviland & Clark, 1974). This arrangement of the construction instructions gives the reader first, the first thing he or she will need—*where* to put the upcoming fact—so she or he can move a mental pointer there—and second, *what* to put there—so he or she can put it there at once.

The first example of a text revision based on the given-new notion in Table 1.4 is in the second sentence with regard to the first sentence. But first we must notice that the second sentence is actually a compound sentence, composed of two separate complete sentences joined by the conjunction "as." So the units involved in this example can be written as:

11. By the fall of 1964, Americans in both Saigon and Washington had begun to focus on Hanoi as the source of the continuing problem in the South.
12. As
13. frustrations mounted over the inability of the ARVN to defeat the enemy in the field,
14. pressure to strike directly at North Vietnam began to build.

How can we rearrange 13 so that (a) the *first* thing mentioned is the old, (given) information, so the learner can move his or her mental pointer to the location in his or her mental representation at which the rest of the sentence should be placed; and (b) the *second* thing mentioned is the new (to-be-added) information? Our first step must be to identify which is the old and which is the new information. In 13, it is clear that "frustrations mounted" has never been mentioned before, so it must be new. And we have seen in the example under Principle 1 that "the inability of the ARVN to defeat the enemy in the field" is actually a repetition of an old idea from

11 (i.e., "the continuing problem in the South"). So the new information must be "frustration mounted" and the old information is "the inability of the ARVN to defeat the enemy in the field" (whereas "over" relates the old to the new by the relation of causality).

In 13, we can see that the new information comes first, and the old comes second. (This happens in 20 other cases in the Original Version.) So the learner encounters the to-be-added information *before* she or he knows where to add it. Our theory proposes that the learner's job would be easier if the person first knew where to go in his or her mental representation; and then, when she or he arrived, procured the next thing needed—the information to be added to that location in his or her mental representation. To help the learner, we should reverse the order of 13 to something like:

15. The inability of the ARVN to defeat the enemy in the field (old) caused frustration (new).

From here, the route to the Principled Revision in Table 1.5 is straightforward. Since *ARVN* is one of the many different terms referring to the South Vietnamese, we changed it to the "South Vietnamese Army." Under Principle 1, we have shown why "the inability of the ARVN to defeat the enemy in the field" was changed to "the South Vietnamese Army was losing the ground war against North Vietnam." Incorporating that revision in 15, we have:

16. the South Vietnamese army was losing the ground war against North Vietnam (old) and this caused frustrations (new).

The adding of the phrase "among the American officials" to this sentence is explained next.

Principle 3. Make coherence easier to establish by making explicit any important implicit references: For instance, when an important concept is referred to implicitly, refer to it explicitly if the reader may otherwise miss an important coherence link.

For example, 13 refers to "frustrations" but does not state who is frustrated. Passive, unmotivated, confused, or overburdened learners may fail to figure out that it must be the "Americans" of the first sentence who are frustrated. The Americans are important players in this text, so we insert the needed information into the text. ("Americans" was changed to "American officials" by Principle 1 because of the 23 different terms used for it.) Similarly, the link between "frustrations" and "pressure" is left implicit in the original version, but made explicit in the Principled Revision.

Other principles were used as well. (See Britton & Gulgoz, 1991; Gulgoz, 1989 for details.)

Heuristic Revision

In addition, the first author constructed a Heuristic Revision, shown in Table 1.6, using his own expertise, which is largely in the form of less easily statable principles, along with rules for the order of application of the principles. At this point, the Heuristic Revision is a heuristic device for theory development: As the expertise becomes articulated, it can be incorporated in the theory.

Readability Formula Revision

Because the Heuristic Revision had readability formula scores about two grades lower than the Original Version, a Readability Formula Revision was also constructed by shortening the longest words and sentences of the Original Version until its readability formula scores were the same as the Heuristic Revision.

Method

One-hundred-seventy undergraduates read one of the versions at their own pace. Three tests were used: free recall, a multiple choice test of information elements that were stated in all versions, and inference questions. The inference questions tested whether readers of the Original Version had themselves inferred, added, and remembered the missing information needed to link the sentences to each other. For the Principled Revision (in which we had inserted the linking information into the text), the inference questions tested whether the learners had remembered it. Separate groups took the free recall and multiple choice test immediately and 24 hours later, but because the pattern of results at both test delays was the same (of course, there were declines in performance due to forgetting) this variable is not considered here for expository simplicity.

Predictions for the Principled Revision. We predicted that the Principled Revision would be retrieved better than the Original on a free recall test. This was because the different parts of the Principled Revision were more likely to be coherently linked to each other, so the learner was more likely to have a retrieval route available to use. This notion is illustrated in Fig. 1.2. The top panel shows the fully linked representation; the bottom shows it with two missing links. Free recall proceeds by passing along links to content element nodes. If a link is missing, the content nodes below it are inaccessible.

On the inference test, learners of the Principled Revision would do better than learners of the Original Version because they would be likely to recognize the added information, which was explicitly presented in their text. (Learners of the Original Version would have had to infer the added information in order to recognize the to-be-inferred information correctly on the inference test.)

But on the multiple choice test of information that was present in all versions, we predicted no advantage for the Principled Revision. Because the information had been explicitly mentioned in the texts, and we always explicitly provided the correct answer as one of the multiple choices, the learner did not have to retrieve the answer from memory but only had to recognize it; so the extra retrieval routes provided by the Principled Revision would not help because retrieval was not called for.

Predictions for the Heuristic Revision. We predicted that the Heuristic Revision would be superior to the Original Version on the free recall test. No prediction was made for reading rate because the Heuristic Revision, although it provided some links, incorporated many other changes whose effects on reading time were unpredictable. No predic-

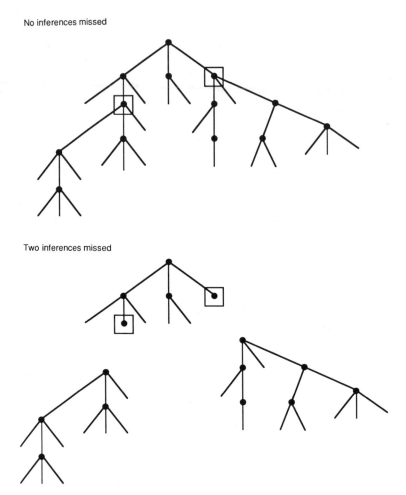

No inferences missed

Two inferences missed

FIG. 1.2 Two hypothetical schematic representations of a text. Inference opportunities are shown by the squares.

tion was made for the inference test because only some links were provided in the Heuristic Revision, whereas the calls for other links were omitted altogether.

Predictions for the Readability Formula Revision. The Readability Formula Revision matched the Heuristic Revision in that it was two grade levels below the Original Version and the Principled Revisions, using five readability formulae. No differences from the Original Version were predicted on any dependent measure.

Results

Table 1.7 shows the results. The tests were one-tailed comparisons against the Original Version. Asterisks are used to indicate significant differences. All the predictions were confirmed. The Principled Revision was recalled significantly better than the Original Version but not recognized better, indicating that more retrieval routes were available to the learner when the links were provided in the text. Inference test performance was significantly better for the Principled Revision than the Original Version, but multiple choice performance was not.

The Heuristic Revision was recognized significantly better than the Original Version on the multiple choice test, indicating it was encoded more correctly and completely. It was also free recalled significantly better than the Original Version. The Readability Formula Revision did not differ from the Original Version on any dependent measures.

Discussion

These results support Kintsch's theory of learning from text, and the conclusion that naturally occurring texts can be improved using the principles of the theory. The Principled Revision is an implementation of the present form of the theory; the Readability Formula Revision represents the main past theory; the Heuristic Revision is a heuristic device

TABLE 1.7
Results of Experiment in Rewriting Text to Improve Learning

	Original Version	Principled Revision	Heuristic Revision	Readability Formula Revision
Free Recall (Number of Propositions)	35.5	58.6*	56.2*	32.8
Multiple Choice Test (Percent correct)	59.4	62.7	68.3*	58.5
Inference Questions (Percent correct)	37.1	46.4*	48.2$^-$	39.7

*different from Original Version, $p < .05$.
$^-$not tested against Original Version.

looking toward the future of the theory. Additional supporting results are reported by Britton, Van Dusen, Glynn, and Hemphill (1990).

IMPLICATIONS FOR TEXTBOOK SELECTORS, PUBLISHERS, AND RESEARCHERS

Citizens, parents, textbook selectors, and researchers all see the same problem: many textbooks are written poorly. It is notable that poor textbooks persist despite the fact that textbook publishers have whole heartedly applied one technique tested by researchers—the use of largely paralinguistic, construction instruction devices such as headings, typographical cues, advanced organizers, summaries, and so on—and the selectors of textbooks have sometimes fallen in behind the publishers by counting these text features and entering the sums into their formulas for selecting textbooks.

As a result of this, many textbooks are copiously studded with these devices (Tyson-Bernstein, 1988). At this point, the use of paralinguistic construction instructions has gone about as far as it can go—no one can accuse the textbook industry of half-hearted efforts in this regard, or of failure to stay the course, or go far enough. But as anyone can see, most textbooks are still very hard to understand and aversive to read.

Why have the results of paralinguistic construction instructions been so disappointing? One reason is a failure of implementation. Consider a text feature like headings. If headings are carefully devised by a knowledgeable researcher who knows that their effectiveness will be tested empirically, they may be effective. What does this imply for headings that are dashed off in a hurry by a textbook production shop on a fixed price contract? It implies nothing at all. That is, carefully constructed headings may be effective in experiments but that does not imply that carelessly constructed ones will be effective in schools.

Another reason for the failure of paralinguistic construction instructions is more simple and basic. Paralinguistic construction instructions cannot substitute for good language in the text; they can only supplement it. If the text itself is unclear, incoherent, and missing important elements or links, the representation of the text will inevitably be incorrect, incomplete, and unretrievable for the average reader, and no amount of paralinguistic construction instructions (even if they are carefully designed) can carry the whole load of clarifying an unclear, incoherent text.

Why Textbooks Are Written Badly

Why are textbooks so often unclear? We argue here that there are three reasons. One reason arises from the fact that the people who write the texts *are* experts in the particular subject matter. The second reason arises from the fact that they are often *not* experts in writing clearly. The third reason is that crippling restrictions are often imposed on the authoring process.

The Effects of Experts' Knowledge Structures. It is perhaps surprising, but unfortunately true, that the experts' subject matter expertise sometimes interferes with clear writing. The reason is because experts' knowledge structures function automatically, so automatically that these structures often are not consciously available to the expert. Instead they are opaque to him or her because they operate so rapidly. This occurred because the expert, because of time restraints, long before had to stop explicitly formulating each mental step in words. But to write a textbook, the expert has to translate his or her expertise into terms that are accessible to the novice. When the expert's own to-be-translated expertise is opaque to him or her because of extended practice, translating the expertise will be difficult.

In other words, the expert has vast amounts of domain relevant prior knowledge, images, and experience, and although all this was once declarative knowledge, it long ago became proceduralized, and so is also largely inaccessible to him or her. But it is needed, and in declarative form, by the novice to take the mental steps that the expert takes automatically and unconsciously. So the expert starts out with two strikes against him or her.

Inexpert Writing. But even if the expert did have easy declarative access to his or her expertise, she or he would still be unable to express this expertise clearly because she or he is often not a good writer. Writing clearly is difficult and time consuming, even for expert writers, as interviews with them illustrate (Plimpton, 1988), and as any writer can testify from personal experience.

Why is it so difficult to effectively write learnable text? It is difficult because the writer has to predict correctly the effect his or her text will have on the mind of the learner. To do this, the writer has to simulate the effect of his or her text on the mind of the learner. The expert has to have, inside the mind, a little model of the target learner's mind, with its mental programs and habits and declarative prior knowledge. Also the writer must have access to a representation of his or her own subject matter expertise—that which she or he is trying to teach.

Then the writer has to invent the elements that could be in his or her text—the content elements and the construction instructions—and arrange them in a particular configuration, using whatever writing ability she or he has. Inventing content elements is hard to do well, and arranging them in an optimal configuration is still a mysterious art. Next, the writer must run that configuration through the mental model he or she has of the intended learner's mind, and see what the result is—a mental representation of the texts meaning in the learner's mind in the case of textbooks. Usually the first draft will not produce the desired memory trace, so the writer will have to reconfigure the elements and run it through again. The process has to be repeated until the memory trace that the writer predicts for the learner is the same as the memory trace that the writer intends to create. Then, if the writer had a correct model of the reader, and was able to run successive drafts of the text through the model *de novo,* and if the writer had correct ideas of what sort of trace is retrievable and was able to invent optimal elements, and so on, only then will the text do the job intended.

No writers do this explicitly, but all writers should do it implicitly if they wish to produce learnable texts. But this process is difficult, time consuming, and uncertain of success. How many textbook writers have the ability to do this, and the time, and how many publishers can afford to pay for this expertise when their competition may be taking the substitute and much cheaper route of simply sprinkling the text with easily countable paralinguistic construction instructions, along with eye-catching illustrations, colorful boxes, and so forth?

Restrictions on Authoring. Often textbook authors are obligated to include something about each item on very long lists of topics mandated by state adoption agencies; or to conform their writing, page by page, to readability formula scores; or to comply with other restrictions and guidelines (Tyson-Bernstein, 1988). But it is difficult enough to write a clear text when one is completely free to use one's own best judgement. To write clearly under detailed restrictions and guidelines is a great deal harder, and may be impossible for all but the most skilled writers. Some textbooks are not written by individuals at all, but by committees, so that no individual's best judgment can be applied at all. Everyone who has dealt with committee constructed documents knows that these documents often have shortcomings.

What Are the Solutions?

The Solution for Textbook Selectors. First, the textbook selectors should keep their "eye on the ball": learning. They should stop focusing on correlates of learning. The textbook selectors should stop counting the letters in words and the words in sentences; readability formulae should be set aside. They should also stop counting the headings, illustrations, and so on.

Instead, the selectors should attend directly to the relative learnability of the various textbooks. We know that there are people who can accurately judge learnability; they should be found and placed into the textbook selection process. If possible, the learnability of alternate texts should be assessed by suitable experimental trials in which learning is measured. But this is so difficult and time consuming that it can rarely be implemented. However, even a few such trials can provide examples of good and poor textbook materials that can be used to select good judges of learnability at each grade level. Such judges should be included in the current textbook selection process.

The Solution for Publishers. Once the textbook selectors focus correctly, the publishers will join in; they are skilled at following the demands of the market. Because the main problem in current textbooks is the writing, the publishers will have to attend to the writing. A few lucky publishers will continue to find subject matter experts who are also expert writers. But the supply of such people is very limited. Just as lucky are the publishers who find good editors, who can help writers write well. The supply of editors is larger, but still limited. A major source of improvement will be the feedback from judgments of learnability gathered by textbook selection committees and by the publishers, and the gradual improvement in writers' and editors' skills that will result from implementing the lessons from that feedback.

The Solution for Researchers. Expert writers and editors can depend on their intuitions; their skills are so well practiced that they are automatic and rapid. But the rest of the writers will have to depend on explicit, articulated knowledge about how to write learnable text. They will have to learn it slowly and painfully, hoping it will gradually become automatized.

This is where the researchers come in. Their task should be to articulate and make explicit the knowledge and mental programs that journeyman writers and editors can use to produce good learnable text. The researchers' tasks are just beginning. Their work should be directed specifically at repairing the problems that subject matter experts have in expressing their knowledge. Earlier in this chapter, we delineated one of these problems in detail: Experts leave out links that are automatic for the expert, but must be spelled out for the novice. This problem arises from the nature of expertise and novicehood. This and other such problems should be investigated.

CONCLUSION

As a result of these actions by textbook selectors, publishers, and researchers, we can hope for a rebirth of clear writing, guided by the findings of cognitive science. For all of human history, learning has been largely a matter of being told. For many eons, this was done by the power of speech.

Text is crystallized speech. For several decades, researchers and educators have been striving to supplement the word; in successive waves, we have had radio, teaching machines, movies, TV, computer-assisted instruction, computer-based instruction, and so on; at the moment, we have interactive-computer tutors and hypertext—all have found their niche or are finding it now. But as each wave advances, breaks, and recedes, what is left behind is the ground on which most education takes place: the power of the word. If the near future of education is the same as the past history of education—in the word—then it is by the understanding and improvement of connective discourse that education can most effectively be advanced.

ACKNOWLEDGMENT

This research was supported by a grant to Bruce K. Britton from the U.S. Air Force Office of Scientific Research, Air Force Human Resources Laboratory, Learning Ability Measurement Project, Grant AFOSR-89-0515.

REFERENCES

Air Force ROTC-ATC. (1985). *U.S. airpower: Key to deterrence.* Montgomery, AL: Maxwell Air Force Base, United States Air Force.

Baumann, J. F. (1986). Effects of rewritten content textbook passages on middle grade students' comprehension of main ideas: Making the inconsiderate considerate. *Journal of Reading Behavior, 18*, 1–21.

Beck, I. L., McKeown, M. G., Omanson, R. C., & Pople, M. T. (1984). Improving the comprehensibility of stories: The effects of revisions that improve coherence. *Reading Research Quarterly, 19*, 263–277.

Brandt, D. M. (1979). Prior knowledge of author's schema and the comprehension of prose. *Dissertation Abstracts International, 39*, 5605B–5606B (University Microfilms No. 79-11113).

Bransford, J. D., & Johnson, M. K. (1972). Contextual prerequisites for understanding: Some investigations of comprehension and recall. *Journal of Verbal Learning and Verbal Behavior, 11*, 717–726.

Brennan, A. D., Bridge, C. A., & Winograd, P. N. (1986). The effects of structural variation on children's recall of basal reader stories. *Reading Research Quarterly, 21*, 91–104.

Britton, B. K., & Gulgoz, S. (1991). Using Kintsch's computational model to improve instructional text: Effects of repairing inference calls on recall and cognitive structures. *Journal of Educational Psychology, 83*, 329–345.

Britton, B. K., Gulgoz, S., Van Dusen, L., Glynn, S. M., & Sharp, L. (1991).

Accuracy of learnability judgments for instructional texts. *Journal of Educational Psychology, 83,* 43–47.

Britton, B. K., & Radford, D. (1988). *Improving biology texts by rewriting.* Unpublished manuscript.

Britton, B. K., Van Dusen, L., Glynn, S. M., & Hemphill, D. (1990). The impact of inferences on instructional text. In A. C. Graesser & G. H. Bower (Eds.), *The psychology of learning and motivation* (Vol. 25, pp. 63–70). New York: Academic Press.

Britton, B. K., Van Dusen, L., & Gulgoz, S. (1991). Reply to "Response to 'Instructional texts rewritten by five expert teams'." *Journal of Educational Psychology, 83,* 149–152.

Britton, B. K., Van Dusen, L., Gulgoz, S., & Glynn, S. M. (1989). Instructional texts rewritten by five expert teams: Revisions and retention improvements. *Journal of Educational Psychology, 81,* 226–239.

Brooks, L. W., Dansereau, D. F., Spurlin, J. E., & Holley, C. D. (1983). Effects of headings on text processing. *Journal of Educational Psychology, 75,* 292–302.

Caplan, L. J., & Schooler, C. (1989). *Analogy and complexity of processing in text comprehension.* Paper presented at the Annual Meeting of the Psychonomic Society, Atlanta, GA.

Christensen, C. M., & Stordahl, K. E. (1955). The effect of organization aids on comprehension and retention. *Journal of Educational Psychology, 46,* 65–74.

Coleman, E. B., (1962). Improving comprehensibility by shortening sentences. *Journal of Applied Psychology, 46,* 131–134.

Cook, N. M. (1981). Summaries: Further issues and data. *Educational Review, 33,* 215–222.

Doctorow, M., Wittrock, M. C., & Marks, C. (1978). Generative processes in reading comprehension. *Journal of Educational Psychology, 70,* 109–118.

Dooling, D. J., & Lachman, R. (1971). Effects of comprehension on retention of prose. *Journal of Experimental Psychology, 88,* 216–222.

Duffy, T. M., Higgins, L., Mehlenbacher, B., Cochran, C., Burnett, R., Wallace, D., Hill, C., Haugen, D., McCaffery, M., Sloane, S., & Smith, S. (1989). Models for the design of instructional text. *Reading Research Quarterly, 24,* 434–457.

Duffy, T. M., & Kabance, P. (1982). Testing a readable writing approach to text revision. *Journal of Educational Psychology, 74,* 733–748.

Fass, W., & Schumacher, G. M. (1978). Effects of motivation, subject activity, and readability on the retention of prose materials. *Journal of Educational Psychology, 70,* 803–807.

Fishman, A. S. (1978). The effect of anaphoric references and noun phrase organizers on paragraph comprehension. *Journal of Reading Behavior, 10,* 159–170.

Foster, J. J. (1979). The use of visual cues in text. In P. A. Kolers, M. E. Wrolstad, & H. Bouma (Eds.), *Processing of visible language* (Vol. 1, pp. 189–203). New York: Plenum.

Freebody, P., & Anderson, R. C. (1983). Effect of vocabulary difficulty, text cohesion and schema availability on reading comprehension. *Reading Research Quarterly, 18,* 277–294.

Givon, T. (in press). The grammar of referential coherence as mental processing instructions. *Cognitive Science.*

Glenberg, A. M., & Epstein, W. (1985). Calibration of comprehension. *Journal of Experimental Psychology: Learning, Memory and Cognition, 11,* 702–708.

Glenberg, A. M., & Epstein, W. (1987). Inexpert calibration of comprehension. *Memory and Cognition, 15,* 84–93.

Glenberg, A. M., Sanocki, T., Epstein, W., & Morris, C. (1987). Enhancing calibration of comprehension. *Journal of Experimental Psychology: General, 116,* 119–136.

Glenberg, A. M., Wilkinson, A. C., & Epstein, W. (1982). The illusion of knowing: Failure in the self-assessment of comprehension. *Memory and Cognition, 10,* 663–679.

Glynn, S. M., & DiVesta, F. J. (1979). Control of prose processing via instructional and typographical cues. *Journal of Educational Psychology, 71,* 595–603.

Graves, M. F., Prenn, M., Earle, J., Thompson, M., Johnson, V., & Slater, W. H. (1990). Commentary: Improving instructional text: Some lessons learned. *Reading Research Quarterly, 26,* 110–122.

Graves, R., & Hodge, A. (1943). *The reader over your shoulder.* New York: Macmillan.

Graves, M. F., & Slater, W. H. (1986). Could textbooks and would textbooks. *American Educator, 10,* 36–42.

Graves, M. F., & Slater, W. H. (1991). A response to "Instructional texts rewritten by five expert teams." *Journal of Educational Psychology, 83,* 147–148.

Graves, M. F., Slater, W. H., Roen, D., Redd-Boyd, T., Duin, A. H., Furniss, D. W., & Hazeltine, P. (1988). Some characteristics of memorable expository writing: Effects of revisions by writers with different backgrounds. *Research in the Teaching of English, 22,* 242–265.

Gulgoz, S. (1989). *Revising text to improve learning: Methods based on text processing models, expertise, and readability formulas.* Unpublished doctoral dissertation, University of Georgia, Athens.

Halliday, M. A. K., & Hasan, R. (1976). *Cohesion in English.* London: Longman.

Hartley, J., Bartlett, S., & Branthwaite, A. (1980). Underlining can make a difference—sometimes. *Journal of Educational Research, 73,* 218–224.

Hartley, J., Goldie, M., & Steen, L. (1979). The role and position of summaries: Some issues and data. *Educational Review, 31,* 59–65.

Hartley, J., Kenely, J., Owen, G., & Trueman, M. (1980). The effect of headings on children's recall of prose text. *British Journal of Education Psychology, 50,* 304–307.

Hartley, J., & Trueman, M. (1985). A research strategy for text designers: The role of headings. *Instructional Science, 14,* 99–155.

Haviland, S. E., & Clark, H. H. (1974). What's new? Acquiring new information as a process of comprehension. *Journal of Verbal Learning and Verbal Behavior, 13,* 512–521.

Hershberger, W. (1964). Self-evaluational responding and typographical cueing: Techniques for programming self-instructional reading materials. *Journal of Educational Psychology, 55,* 288–296.

Hershberger, W., & Terry, D. F. (1965). Typographical cuing in conventional and programmed texts. *Journal of Applied Psychology, 49,* 55–60.

Hidi, S., & Baird, W. (1988). *The effect of structural revisions on learning from school texts.* Unpublished manuscript, Ontario Institute for Studies in Education: Center for Applied Cognitive Science, Toronto.

Holley, C. D., Dansereau, D. F., Evans, S. H., Collins, K. W., Brooks, L., & Larson, D. (1981). Utilizing intact and embedded headings as processing aids with nonnarrative text. *Contemporary Educational Psychology, 6,* 227–236.

Keenan, J. M., Baillet, S. D., & Brown, P. (1984). The effects of causal cohesion on comprehension and memory. *Journal of Verbal Learning and Verbal Behavior, 23,* 115–126.

Kern, R. P., Sticht, T. G., Welty, D., & Hauke, R. N. (1976). *Guidebook for the development of Army training literature.* Alexandria, VA: Human Resources Research Organization.

Kieras, D. E. (1978). Good and bad structure in simple paragraphs: Effects on apparent theme, reading time, and recall. *Journal of Verbal Learning and Verbal Behavior, 17,* 13–28.

Kintsch, E. (1990). Macroprocesses and microprocesses in the development of summarization skill. *Cognition & Instruction, 7,* 161–195.

Kintsch, W., & van Dijk, T. A. (1978). Toward a model of text comprehension and production. *Psychological Review, 85,* 363–394.

Kintsch, W., & Yarbrough, J. C. (1982). Role of rhetorical structure in text comprehension. *Journal of Educational Psychology, 74,* 828–834.

Klare, G. R. (1963). *The measurement of readability.* Ames: Iowa State University Press.

Klare, G. R., Mabry, J. E., & Gustafson, L. M. (1955). The relationship of patterning (underlining) to immediate retention and to acceptability of technical material. *Journal of Applied Psychology, 39,* 40–42.

Kniffin, J. D., Stevenson, C. R., Klare, G. R., Entin, E., Slaughter, S., & Hooke, L. (1979). *Operational consequences of a literacy gap* (AFHRL-TR-79-22). Brooks Air Force Base, TX: Air Force Human Resources Laboratory. (NTIS No. AD A084 782/2).

Loman, N. L., & Mayer, R. (1983). Signaling techniques that increase the understandability of expository prose. *Journal of Educational Psychology, 75,* 402–412.

Lorch, R. F. (1989). Text signaling devices and their effects on reading and memory processes. *Educational Psychology Review, 1,* 209–234.

Lorch, R. F., Jr. (1985). Effects on recall of signals to text organization. *Bulletin of the Psychonomic Society, 23,* 374–376.

Lorch, R. F., Jr., & Chen, A. H. (1986). Effects of number signals on reading and recall. *Journal of Educational Psychology, 78,* 263–270.

Lorch, R. F., & Lorch, E. P. (1985). Topic structure representation and text recall. *Journal of Educational Psychology, 77,* 137–148.

Maki, R. H., & Berry, S. L. (1987). Metacomprehension of text material. *Journal of Experimental Psychology: Learning, Memory, and Cognition, 10,* 663–679.

Mannes, S. M., & Kintsch, W. (1987). Knowledge organization and text organization. *Cognition and Instruction, 4,* 91–115.

Marshall, N., & Glock, M. D. (1978–79). Comprehension of connected discourse: A study into the relationships between the structure of text and *information recalled. Reading Research Quarterly, 14,* 10–56.

Mayer, R. E. (1983). Can you repeat that? Qualitative effects of repetition and advance organizers on learning from science prose. *Journal of Educational Psychology, 75,* 40–49.

Mayer, R. E., Cook, L. K., & Dyck, J. L. (1984). Techniques that help readers build mental models from scientific text: Definitions pretraining and signaling. *Journal of Educational Psychology, 76,* 1089–1105.

McCracken, R. A. (1959). An experiment with contrived readability in fifth and sixth grades. *Journal of Educational Research, 52,* 277–278.

McDonald, D. R. (1987). *Drawing inferences from expository text.* Unpublished doctoral dissertation, New Mexico State University, Las Cruces.

Meyer, B. J. F., Brandt, D. M., & Bluth, G. J. (1980). Use of top-level structure in text: Key for reading comprehension of ninth-grade students. *Reading Research Quarterly, 16,* 72–103.

Meyer, B. J. F., & Freedle, R. O. (1984). Effects of discourse type on recall. *American Educational Research Journal, 21,* 121–143.

Miller, J. R., & Kintsch, W. (1980). Readability and recall of short prose passages: A theoretical analysis. *Journal of Experimental Psychology: Human Learning and Memory, 6,* 335–354.

Mohr, P., Glover, J. A., & Ronning, R. R. (1984). The effect of related and unrelated details on the recall of major ideas in prose. *Journal of Reading Behavior, 16,* 97–108.

Parker, J. P. (1962). Some organizational variables and their effect upon comprehension. *Journal of Communication, 12,* 27–32.

Pepper, J. (1981). Following students' suggestions for rewriting a computer programming textbook. *American Educational Research Journal, 18,* 259–269.

Phifer, S. J., McNickle, B., Ronning, R. R., & Glover, J. A. (1983). The effect of details on the recall of major ideas in text. *Journal of Reading Behavior, 15,* 19–30.

Plimpton, G. (1986). *Writers at work: The Paris Review interviews.* New York: Viking.

Reder, L. M., & Anderson, J. R. (1980). A comparison of texts and their summaries: Memorial consequences. *Journal of Verbal Learning and Verbal Behavior, 19,* 121–134.

Reder, L. M., & Anderson, J. R. (1982). Effects of spacing and embellishments on memory for the main points of a text. *Memory and Cognition, 10,* 97–102.

Roen, D. H., & Piche, G. L. (1984). The effects of selected text-forming structures on college freshmen's comprehension of expository prose. *Research in the Teaching of English, 18,* 8–25.

Schallert, D. L. (1976). Improving memory for prose: The relationship between depth of processing and context. *Journal of Verbal Learning and Verbal Behavior, 15,* 621–632.

Schommer, M., & Surber, J. R. (1986). Comprehension monitoring failure in skilled adult readers. *Journal of Educational Psychology, 78,* 353–357.

Schwartz, M. N. V., & Flammer, A. (1981). Text structure and title—effects on comprehension and recall. *Journal of Verbal Learning and Verbal Behavior, 20,* 61–66.

Shebilske, W. L., & Rotondo, J. A. (1981). Typographical and spatial cues that facilitate learning from textbooks. *Visible Language, 15,* 41–54.

Siegel, A. I., Lambert, J. V., & Burkett, J. R. (1974). *Techniques for making written material more readable/comprehensible* (AFHRL-TR-74-47). Lowry Air Force Base, CO: Air Force Human Resources Laboratory, Technical Training Division. (NTIS No. AD 786 849).

Slater, W. H. (1985). Revising inconsiderate elementary school expository text: Effects on comprehension and recall. In J. Niles & R. V. Lavik (Eds.), *Issues in literacy: A research perspective* (pp. 186–193). Rochester, NY: National Reading Conference.

Slater, W. H., Graves, M. F., & Piche, G. L. (1985). Effects of structural organizers on ninth-grade students' comprehension and recall of four patterns of expository text. *Reading Research Quarterly, 20,* 189–202.

Slater, W. H., Palmer, R. J., & Graves, M. F. (1982). Effects of directions describing passage structure, signaling, and elaboration on readers' recall. *Research on Reading in Secondary Schools, 9*(2), 1–25.

Spyridakis, J. H., & Standal, T. C. (1986). Headings, previews, logical connectives: Effects on reading comprehension. *Journal of Technical Writing and Communication, 16,* 343–354.

Spyridakis, J. H., & Standal, T. C. (1987). Signals in expository prose: Effects on reading comprehension. *Reading Research Quarterly, 22,* 285–298.

Swaney, J. H., Janik, C. J., Bond, S. J., & Hayes, J. R. (1981). *Editing for comprehension: Improving the process through reading protocols* (Tech. Rep. No. 14). Pittsburgh, PA: Document Design Project.

Tenenbaum, A. B. (1977). Task-dependent effects of organization and context upon comprehension of prose. *Journal of Educational Psychology, 69,* 528–536.

Tidwell, P. S. (1989). *Improving written material: An empirical test of passages revised by E. D. Hirsch.* Unpublished master's thesis, University of Georgia, Athens.

Tyson-Bernstein, H. (1988). *A conspiracy of good intentions: America's textbook fiasco.* Washington, DC: Council for Basic Education.

van Dijk, T. A., & Kintsch, W. (1983). *Strategies of discourse comprehension.* New York: Academic Press.

Walczyk, J. J., & Hall, V. C. (1989). Effects of examples and embedded questions on the accuracy of comprehension self-assessments. *Journal of Educational Psychology, 81,* 435–437.

Weaver, C. A. (1990). Constraining factors in calibration of comprehension. *Journal of Experimental Psychology: Learning, Memory & Cognition, 16,* 214–222.

Wilhite, S. C. (1986). The relationship of headings, questions, and locus of control to multiple-choice test performance. *Journal of Reading Behavior, 18,* 23–39.

Williams, J. P., Taylor, M. B., & Ganger, S. (1981). Text variations at the level of the individual sentence and the comprehension of simple expository paragraphs. *Journal of Educational Psychology, 73,* 851–865.

Young, S. R. (1984). A theory and simulation of macrostructure (Tech. Rep. No. 134). Boulder, CO: Institute of Cognitive Science, University of Colorado.

Zabrucky, K. (1986). The role of factual coherence in discourse comprehension. *Discourse Processes, 9,* 197–220.

Zipf, G. K. (1949). *Human behavior and the principle of least effort.* Cambridge, MA: Addison-Wesley.

— ■ 2 ■ —

Questioning Questions in Teaching and Learning From Texts

Richard L. Allington
Rose-Marie Weber
State University of New York at Albany

Perhaps Thorndike (1917) is primarily to blame for our preoccupation with questioning. His classic study contributed substantially to the notion that comprehension and learning from texts could be derived by questioning. The study was designed to illustrate that even though students could read text aloud accurately, they did not necessarily understand the facts or the principles expressed in the material. By using questions to measure comprehension, Thorndike not only provided the basis for a widely adopted research method but also the most common format in the development of standardized tests of reading comprehension. Asking questions during and after reading became prevalent practice for assessing comprehension during reading instruction and, over time, the accepted strategy for fostering comprehension (Allington, 1983).

Thorndike, however, was not demonstrating the possibilities of a particularly novel approach. Rather, his work reflected a long-standing practice, because the place of questions in textbooks was by that time well established and, as Dillon (1982) traced, was strongly supported by emerging educational theories. The value of questions, it was argued, was in their capacity for stimulating thought processes. For instance, in a book written for school administrators and teachers around the time of Thorndike's paper, *The Textbook: How to Use and Judge It,* Hall-Quest (1920) saw the textbook as a guide, as a source of knowledge, as a means of interpreting truth, and as an incentive to inspiration. He included a set of questions and problems for each of the volume's nine chapters. In his view, questions and problems were important in two respects: "They make reviewing convenient, but their chief value lies in stimulating the pupil to apply what he has studied and to think out the solution of the problems suggested by the author, especially if these problems refer to matters in which the pupil is personally interested" (pp. 131, 132). He asked, "What percent of questions in your textbooks are thought-provoking and vital?" (p. 155).

Thorndike's operationalization of "comprehension as question answering" in research provided an impetus for the use of questions to foster comprehension during reading instruction. Whereas questions had been used to assess comprehension for some time, it was during Thorndike's era that question asking became accepted as instruction. Although he may not have meant to recommend questioning as a way to foster comprehension, Thorndike's recommendation (and the similar recommendations of others) that silent reading, followed by questions, replace oral reading seems to have produced that effect. Venezky (1986) argued that the existence of questions in early reading materials (before 1900) indicates that traditional interpretations, those that suggest comprehension was not a focus of early reading instruction (Smith, 1968), are inaccurate. We would suggest that a shift did occur between 1900 and 1925, but the shift was in the perceived function of questions during and after reading. Although questions after stories were common in the early readers, it was not until about 1920 that publishers offered teacher's manuals with lesson outlines for each story, and, shortly thereafter, offered workbook-like ancillary materials to accompany the readers. These two additions to the product line were the result of attempts to shift the emphasis of school reading activity from oral elocution to silent reading comprehension (Langer & Allington, 1992). Furthermore, it seems clear that the questions offered in the teacher's manuals and many of the activities in the workbooks were seen to play an instructional role in fostering the development of comprehension abilities. The reading lesson was formalized with the directed reading activity (Woodward, 1986)—a lesson structure predicated on what might be called the "practice makes perfect" model of instruction. Thus, the use of questions before, during, and after reading was viewed as an appropriate paradigm for facilitating comprehension.

We would like to scrutinize this conventional wisdom that question asking is an appropriate paradigm for facilitating the comprehension of text or fostering learning from them. Although casual acceptance is a hallmark of conventional wisdom and casual acceptance of question asking is a hallmark of both comprehension pedagogy and research, there exist good reasons for a close examination of the use of questions to develop and assess understanding. Primary among these are the development of constructivist and transactional views of the comprehension process and sociocognitive models of the teaching and learning process. Until recently, Thorndike and most who followed him drew upon associationist views of teaching, learning, and comprehending text. Even today, there is much in the design of textbooks that flows directly from this associationist base (Shannon, 1988), including the use of questions as an almost singular method for attempting to foster comprehension.

In this chapter, we refer to research on questioning with respect to teaching reading comprehension in elementary classrooms, and to cumulative research on questioning that draws generalizations about fostering comprehension across subject matters, especially at the upper elementary, secondary, and college levels. These are the domains where there has been the most research. But we should point out that, like others (e.g., Andre, 1987), we see the need for thinking about the purposes, types, and effectiveness of questions—and alternatives to questions—with respect to specific subject areas (e.g., biology, American History, economics). This is important, because an aspect of expertise in a particular area is knowledge of the kinds and questions and answers that are appropriate to it (Andre, 1987, p. 61; see also Armbruster Anderson, Bruning, & Meyer, 1984).

CURRENT USES OF QUESTIONS

Questions abound in textbooks and are generally considered an essential textbook characteristic. From primary grade readers to college texts on the teaching of reading, there are postreading questions printed in the student reading material. These questions are designed to be used throughout or at the end of stories or chapters; they are intended as a basis for recitation or discussion lessons, as guides for independent study, or for written assignments. In many cases, especially in basal reader series, questions about the text also appear in teacher's editions and in workbooks. In addition, today, the teachers' editions typically provide a range of acceptable answers for the questions found in each of the materials (pupil books, teachers' manuals, and workbooks).

Whereas pupil readers have contained questions for a long time, both the modern teacher manual and student workbook are relatively recent additions to commercial curriculum materials. Obviously, the inclusion of questions in these ancillary components is also recent. The current situation is such that question asking by the teacher dominates reading lessons in the elementary school and many content classes in middle and secondary school. It is not the case that pupils are simply presented five questions to answer after reading. Rather, questions to prepare pupils to read, to "guide" their reading, and to deepen their appreciation or understanding, are found in the readers, teacher manuals, workbooks, and other seatwork materials. Although publishers often categorize these questions according to some "level-of-processing" scheme (literal vs. inferential; main idea vs. sequence), the sheer number of questions that are posed outweighs the potential the questions might have for helping children become better comprehenders. But what, outside of conventional wisdom, leads us to believe that asking as many questions as possible will foster independent comprehension?

Another way to consider the issue is to ponder how many "good" questions can one ask about a six-page story or expository section, especially in elementary school readers where texts of 64 (or even 816) words in length are standard fare? The vast majority of questions posed in the various components of instructional materials are single answer questions; that is, the teacher is provided an answer key detailing appropriate responses. Goodman, Shannon, Freeman, and Murphy (1988) provide an analysis of one basal reading series and indicate that from 63% to 98% of all questions posed had single answers keyed as correct (Grade 1 the 63%, Grade 5 had the 98%). In a similar vein, Woodward (1986) noted that basal reader questions not only have answers provided for the teacher but the quantity of these questions seems high and quality low. Tyson-Bernstein (1988) arrived at a similar conclusion concerning other school texts. Current curriculum materials abound with questions for pupils to answer. The teachers' manuals are loaded with questions for teachers to pose to pupils and the answers they are to accept from them. All this is in service of the goal of fostering comprehension through repeated practice of responding to questions targeted at particular comprehension skills.

Given the plentitude of questions offered in the commercial curriculum materials and the emphasis placed in teacher training textbooks on posing questions (e.g., different levels of questions, wait time, etc.), we should not be surprised to find that questions after reading are common in classrooms (e.g., Davey, 1988; Durkin, 1984). It is often the case that young children spend more time responding to questions during instructional sessions than they do reading (Gambrell, 1984; Lalik & Pecic, 1984; Wendler, Samuels, & Moore, 1989). Similarly, in secondary school content area classes, students may spend more time responding to oral or written questions than in text reading (Goodlad, 1984).

However, how teachers use the questions made available to them in textbooks seems to defy generalization. The principles that teachers may follow, consciously or not and consistently, or not, in rejecting, choosing, reordering, modifying, or supplementing the questions in relation to the subject matter, the students, and their intentions are among the little understood complexities of teachers' daily lives. At a time when the potential for teacher-proof texts was a topic of concern, Cronbach (1955) remarked, "The sheer absence of trustworthy fact regarding the-text-in-use is amazing" (p. 216). He also suggested that such study cannot be approached simply because "the text-in-use is a complex social process wherein a book, an institution, and a number of human beings are interlaced beyond the possibility of separation" (p. 188). Unfortunately, his remarks have been largely ignored, and today we find that there are only a few studies that have examined how teachers and students use questions provided by textbooks.

The findings of these studies show variation in practice, but hardly the basis for the variation. In one example, Durkin (1984) observed how teachers in Grades 1, 3, and 5 followed the instructions offered in basal reader manuals and elicited their reasons for using, altering, or rejecting the recommendations to use those instructions. It was with respect to questions after reading that Durkin noted the most dedication to the manuals. All 16 teachers used them, at times in written form after silent reading rather than in spoken form, and sometimes in a different order from what was presented in the manual. Similarly, we have observed teachers in small reading group sessions tracking each and every question laid out for them in the teachers' manual. On the other hand, also in accord with our observations, a group of second grade teachers chose only 20% of the questions they asked during reading group from the manuals, choosing to follow instead their own inclinations, logic, and the children's responses to jointly reconstruct and evaluate events in the stories (Shake & Allington, 1985). A casual inspection of the transcripts suggested that the teachers turned to the manual questions when the momentum of their own questions on a topic or event subsided and they needed a fresh topic.

Shannon (1988) offered an explanation for the variation in adherence to the questions and other suggestions found in teachers manuals, and his findings are generally supported by those reported by Stuetzel (1988). Shannon located a source of variation in administrative press for program implementation. He offered evidence that, when administrators pressed for accountability, many teachers responded by closely adhering to the program manuals and materials. Teachers who did not exhibit a strong sense of personal efficacy in teaching reading were more likely to see commercially prepared curricular materials as "scientific" and were more likely to adhere to recommended practices; this may account for the recent proliferation and popularity of teaching guides and workbooks designed to be used with children's tradebooks. Such materials seem most often found in the classrooms of teachers who are moving away from the traditional basal reading series as general curriculum.

The design of commercial curriculum materials, however, is not the only source of variation in teachers' use of questions. Some kinds of questions deemed important by teachers on a particular occasion cannot be anticipated in textbooks.

Rather, they arise from the progress of the lesson. O'Flaha-van, Hartman, and Pearson (1988) examined a large set of questions in second-, fourth-, and sixth-grade reading com-prehension lessons with respect to how they related to the materials that the children read. Although they did not track how the questions related to the manuals, they determined whether the answer to the question could be found literally in the text or if it could be inferred from information in the text. They also determined if it required the children to turn to their own knowledge, as in this example:

Teacher: . . . what kind of illness did he get. . . ?
Student 1: Laryngitis.
Teacher: Laryngitis. And what is laryngitis? . . .
Student 2: . . . when you can't talk; when your voice is
    gone . . . (p. 197)

One would not expect such questions to appear in a manual, at least as questions designed for after reading, but teachers may want to raise such information so as to insure that students will have the information to draw the appropriate inferences that make a story coherent. Citing the research showing that background knowledge contributes to compre-hension, O'Flahavan, Hartman, and Pearson reported that about 25% of the teachers in their study frequently asked such questions.

Such findings point up the lack of specific concern for the overall course of questioning in relation to a given text within a lesson or, for that matter, over a sequence of lessons. Questions tend to be viewed as individual, free-standing units, not only in textbooks, but in teacher training and research as well. In the case of elementary reading instruc-tion, questions have been traditionally valued as the means for teaching skills such as recognizing the main idea or drawing conclusions (Rosenshine, 1980). Such a perspective does not lend itself to taking into account how questions may be related to one another logically, how subsequent questions the teacher poses might differ, depending on a student's response, or how such questions might shift in purpose and quality as a lesson progresses. Given the current expanded view on the nature of texts and how they are understood, it has been recommended that questions follow the structure of stories and thereby take into account the causal relations among states, characters, motives, and events (e.g., Pearson, 1984; Sadow, 1982). Questions such as these that reconstruct the central content are, however, considered only the basis for further questions exploring the interpretations, esthetic quality, and the like. Other aspects of the relations among questions have been addressed, but only infrequently, in the research that describes the course of reading comprehension lessons, for instance, Au and Kawakami's (1984) detailed analysis of shifts in the functions of questions throughout a given lesson and Collins' (1987) examination of how teachers take up student responses as they ask one question after another. Although Farrar (1986) has emphasized the importance of considering the context in analyses of questions in educational research, this advice, like Cronbach's, for the most part has been ignored.

We offer this overview in an attempt to emphasize that there is a long history of the use of questions after reading, but there is limited information concerning the questions asked by teachers or posed in textbooks in classrooms at all grade levels. It is against this background that we propose to question much of the conventional wisdom that surrounds the use of questions after reading; not only notions about the instructional functions of questions, but also the related use of questions in research on learning and comprehension. In our view, questions have come to occupy a rarely examined function in both teaching and research. Rather than continue the debates about which level of questions, or the appropriate frequency of questions, or the placement of questions, we would question their continued use. We simply examine whether questions fulfill any of the supposed functions that conventional wisdom would suggest.

DO QUESTIONS FACILITATE COMPREHENSION?

Although research, recommended practice, casual observation, and cultural expectations attest to the constancy of questions posed by teachers and textbooks in classrooms, relatively few studies have examined the effects of questions on students' learning. Do they help students understand what they read? Do questions help students learn a broad view as well as the specifics of academic subjects? Do they assist in remembering, integrating, elaborating, and applying information? Do the masses of questions asked in classrooms offer a model of inquiry that truly fosters constructive thinking about the content of textbooks and encourages new learning? Presumably, the questions provide a means for confirming and integrating what students have just read, as well as correcting or refining what they may have otherwise missed.

Several lines of inquiry have examined the effectiveness of questioning experimentally. One line traces the questioning that teachers carry out in classrooms with groups of children, especially at the elementary school level. Although the experimental studies are not directly tied to the use of textbooks, they essentially represent the recitation lesson, a series of teacher questions that, in practice, usually focuses on text content and may be selected from a teacher's guide (Cuban, 1984; Tharp & Gallimore, 1989). Given the widespread practice, it is notable that few researchers have asked the basic question "Would students learn as much if teachers did not use the recitation method to help them review a section of the textbook that they have just read?" (Gall, 1984, p. 44).

In one of these few examples, Gall et al. (1978) designed a study to evaluate the effects of questioning on learning an ecology unit by sixth graders over 10 roughly 50-minute sessions. The research group (a) organized reading and visual materials, (b) prepared scripts of questions for teachers, (c) trained the teachers to use those specific questions and no others, and (d) administered an array of outcome measures to compare four treatments. The first three treatments, in fact, showed no differences among themselves in achievement. That is, whether a group of students was asked content questions, along with probe questions, and questions redirected to other students; whether a group was asked just content questions; or whether a group was asked content questions and provided with some "filler" activities like crossword puzzles did not matter to their achievement in mastering content. But the three groups all exceeded a fourth group who, after reading or viewing materials, were not asked any questions at all but, rather, participated in art activities related to the content of the materials. So, we know

that engagement in question answering produces more correct answers to posttest questions than does engagement in
related art activities. But what of other alternatives that
might delve more deeply into texts (e.g., graphic displays of
content such as semantic webs and time lines, or student
critiques of content, structure, or theme)?

Another line of inquiry regarding the effectiveness of questioning concerns the use of adjunct questions, that is, written
questions that are added to texts in order to influence learning. They essentially reflect the questions that appear in
textbooks or in workbooks and often require a written response. It should be noted that the majority of the studies on
adjunct questions have been conducted with college and
secondary students (Hamaker, 1986), so that the instructional implications for younger students' learning are not
clear. In these studies, however, the effects of questions
versus no questions is rarely addressed. An exception is
Spring, Sassenrath, and Ketellapper's (1986) effort to vali-
date adjunct questions in the realistic setting of a one-quarter
introductory college biology course. Adjunct questions based
on the textbook were prepared at the rate of about two a page.
In the first part of the quarter, half the students were required
to answer the questions in writing whereas the other half did
not receive the questions. (In the second half of the quarter,
the students traded places.) The results were mildly positive
in favor of questions. However, the findings were so slim that
the research group could muster only "guarded optimism"
as to the value of the questions when students used them to
review material that they had read.

A good deal of the research has concerned itself with the
effects of answering questions on the types of learning that
students later demonstrate on criterion tests. The distinction
is drawn between learning content that is directly addressed
by the original study questions and learning content that is
incidental to them, as measured by test questions that repeat, rephrase, or deal with different content. In general,
adjunct postquestions (those appearing after a stretch of
text), have been credited over a range of studies with facilitating prose learning as measured on criterion tests. Presumably, these adjunct postquestions stimulate learners to attend to, reflect on, and integrate the information in the texts
assigned (Andre, 1987). The facilitation definitely shows up

in superior performance on test questions that repeat, or are related to, adjunct questions on facts appearing in the text. But, as Hamaker (1986, 1989) documented from his meta-analysis of adjunct questions studies, facilitation does not show up with respect to learning facts that are unrelated to adjunct questions. This conclusion, however, runs counter to earlier reviews (see Andre, 1987) and points up the fragility of the research support for such questioning strategies. All this suggests to us that the effects of adjunct questioning are too often limited to the content that is highlighted by the questions and, therefore, do not typically result in the deeper and broader processing that educators might often hope for.

Interestingly, the most intense line of experimental research on the effectiveness of questioning has focused on the differences between so-called lower- and higher-level questions. Lower-level questions are generally characterized as those that require students to recall and reiterate literally what they have read or heard. In contrast, higher-level questions are viewed as those that require more complex cognitive operations; that is, drawing information together, applying a concept, explaining, analyzing, evaluating. The conventional wisdom seems to be that higher-level questions will stimulate deeper and more elaborate thinking that results in long-lasting academic achievement than will low-level questions. Even on the basis of descriptive studies, researchers who have found that teachers ask more literal questions than other question types will go on to encourage teachers to ask more higher-level questions (e.g., Guszak, 1967).

Experimental research, however, has not provided steadfast support for the use of higher-level questions, although much work has been undertaken to test their value. The studies generally ask whether a preponderance of higher level questions instead of lower level questions will lead to more effective learning as measured by achievement tests. In some such cases, the lessons are tightly scripted and questions may be set by the experimenters so as to maintain control over the course and content of the questioning (e.g., Gall et al., 1978). The evidence, in this case, is again inconsistent. Studies of such questioning patterns in classrooms, as reviewed, not only in narratives, but also through meta-analysis (e.g., Gall, 1984; Redfield & Rousseau, 1981) suggest that effects are rare and difficult to replicate. For instance, although Redfield and Rousseau (1981) reported that their meta-analytic study yielded a large effect size in favor of higher-level questioning, Samson, Strykowski, Weinstein, and Walberg (1987) could not replicate their findings and rather had to conclude "that large, consistent effects remain to be demonstrated" (p. 294). Meta-analyses of the effects of different levels of adjunct questions also suggest only a small effect, at best (e.g., Andre, 1987; Hamaker, 1986).

Wixson (1983) evaluated the limitations of lower-level questions during the teaching of reading in elementary schools in the context of shifts in thinking about comprehension, brought about by schema theory and concomitant shifts in terminology that distinguish between text-explicit questions as a particular type of lower-level question, and text-implicit questions that require inferences based on the text. Wixson took the view that the interactions between questions and a learner's responses result in modifications to the learner's existing knowledge structure; in this case, the knowledge established by reading a passage. When she compared a group who had been asked text-explicit questions to a group who had received text-implicit questions, she found the latter group of children produced a higher proportion of inferences during recall, yet without loss of explicit information from the text.

What we lack, in this case, and most other areas of questioning research, is any form of truly longitudinal evidence of effects. Far too many studies are only few weeks long, and even those of longer durations rarely extend beyond a single semester. Despite this, studies are too often taken as evidence that some adaptation of the intervention design should be integrated into curriculum materials across a much longer span of time. For instance, the use of higher-level questions or questions generated from a story map are but two examples of research that have been adapted for use in basal reading series. In this case, curriculum inclusion will typically span from Grade 1 to Grade 8, not for a 3-week period, or even a semester. The use of questioning takes time, time that could be spent involving students in other activities such as writing, additional reading, or discussion. We know more, it seems, about the limited effects of various questioning schemes than we do about using the time to engage learners in other instructional activities. In short, we have little consistent evidence about appropriate variations on questioning in the instructional setting and virtually no evidence of the long-term effects of such interventions on the comprehension processes of learners.

ARE ANSWERS TO QUESTIONS EVIDENCE OF COMPREHENSION?

We have too few comparisons of questioning–answering with other postreading tasks that might be viewed as demonstrating comprehension of the material. However, we do have evidence such as that provided by Cole and Griffin (1987). They reported a case study of an adolescent involved in remedial reading instruction, which illustrates that accurate question answering does not necessarily reflect an adequate organization of the content read. Their student could answer postreading questions without acquiring the gist of the text. Similarly, Taylor, Olson, Prenn, Rybczynski, and Zakaluk (1985) demonstrated that children who could complete the common worksheet comprehension task of selecting a main idea statement after reading were no more successful in providing written summaries of social studies materials than students who were unable to complete the main idea task.

Recent data from the National Assessment of Educational Progress (Applebee, Langer, & Mullis, 1988) seem also to illustrate that question answering is not a good indication of performance on other measures of comprehension and understanding. Although the majority of students performed adequately, and many admirably, on multiple-choice questions that followed reading passages, far fewer were able to perform at satisfactory levels when asked to summarize or interpret passages and explain or defend their responses. The performance of the students assessed was summarized thusly, "These findings are disturbing . . . students in American schools can read with surface understanding, but have difficulty when asked to think more deeply about what they have read, to defend or elaborate upon their ideas, and to communicate them in writing" (p. 25).

It may be, as Andre (1987) argued, that practice on certain types of tasks produces reading/learning routines that are powerful, but, at the same time, fairly narrowly focused. Conventional wisdom has often understood question-answering performance as a proxy for performance on other comprehension tasks, but with scant evidence that such a relationship exists. Instead, performance on one question-answering task has often been correlated with performance on other question-answering tasks; it may well be that repeated exposure to question-answering tasks produces students who are better able to answer questions. But even if this is so, we should not assume that the ability to answer questions will lead to improved performance on other comprehension tasks and especially on tasks that require students to organize, summarize, or evaluate materials read.

In accepting the conventional wisdom that question-answering is evidence of comprehension, we may have confused the ability to locate or remember information with understanding (Allington & Strange, 1979). Much of what passes for comprehension assessment (and instruction) requires pupils to simply locate and list information found in text. For instance, most standardized tests of reading comprehension and most comprehension tasks found in curriculum materials allow review and rereading of the text, which is the source of the information queried. Most items on these assessments tap surface information, not interpretations of text, nor elaborations on the information presented. Students are not typically asked to defend or explain their responses. Similarly, the assessments generated by classroom teachers seem to feature memory for discrete items of information found in the text under study (Goodlad, 1984). Perhaps it is because of this that we know more about facilitating pupils question answering than we know about fostering their comprehension.

HOW POSTREADING QUESTIONING MAY LIMIT LEARNING

The established place of questions in textbooks and traditional lessons contributes to the generally held notion that the teacher and textbook—rather than the learner—are uniquely invested with the authority to ask questions.

Writing the answers to homework questions or responding to classroom questions, which the teacher selected from a textbook or teacher manual, may largely define the students' practice of interpreting and learning from texts. The predominant instructional cycles of teachers' questions, students' responses, and teachers' evaluations of these responses create classroom questioning routines that are so highly structured that they are limited to questions set by convention for checking understanding, reviewing content of a text, and eliciting minor interpretations of characters and events (Weber, 1986). The routines do not allow for questions that reveal ignorance, request clarification, puzzle over meaning, express curiosity, draw comparisons, or raise hypotheses on the part of either students or teachers. Although the questions may be thought provoking and vital from the point of view of textbook writers and the teachers depending on them, their remoteness from student interests on particular occasions may have the result of setting limits to the possibilities learners expect of themselves in general.

Further, descriptive studies focusing on minority students suggest that traditional questioning practice, rather than facilitating learning, may set up barriers to it. Heath (1982), for instance, detailed the ways in which questions in classrooms, which analyze phenomena and ask about essential characteristics, sustained the conventional patterns of questioning for mainstream children but broke with the patterns that Black children from a southeastern mill community brought to school. In particular, the teachers' practice of asking children known-answer questions to have them pay attention, label, enumerate characteristics, and pick apart stories they have just read and understood did not make sense to those children who were accustomed to questions requesting information and eliciting analogies. In a different vein, teachers and researchers working with children of Hawaiian descent (e.g., Tharp & Gallimore, 1989) came to realize the restrictions placed on the children's participation by the turn-taking mold implicitly set by long-term mainstream practice and sustained by the use of questions in teachers' manuals. They felt frustrated by the children's resistance and seemingly chaotic responses to standard comprehension questions. When they recognized children's cooperative ways of talking with one another and legitimized it in lessons, the teachers found that they could nurture children's capacities for reviewing and interpreting stories.

The potential benefits of such shifts in instructional practice are not limited to students from minority populations. A number of recent studies have begun to address the use of alternatives to the traditional recitation lesson (e.g., Alvermann & Hayes, 1989; Hansen, 1987; Langer, 1986). In these studies, there was an attempt to capitalize on the curiosity of children. As such, the instructional environments looked quite different from the traditional classrooms; students began formulating questions as they read and wrote. In traditional classrooms, there has been a singular predominance of procedural questions from students ("Do we color it in?" "How many pages do we have to write?" "Which problems do we do?"); whereas, in these experimental settings, student questions reflected more of their curiosity about the topics they studied (Lindfors, 1987). The shifts in classroom environments often resulted in shifts in learning, with students responding to texts in deeper and broader ways, but such change has not come easily, if at all.

Finally, postreading questions may limit learning by reducing the time available to simply continue reading. Given the substantial quantities of time across the school day that students are reported to be spending responding to questions (oral and written), what might be the effect of spending that time engaged in additional reading on the topic? In some cases, student opportunity to read would expand more than twofold. For instance, imagine a tenth-grade American History class where students spend most of their classtime and homework time reading beyond the textbook—reading biographies, historical fiction, and, perhaps, original texts from the era under study. Would reading twice as much text limit comprehension of the content any more than time spent responding to postreading or adjunct questions?

WHAT IF QUESTIONS WERE AUTHENTIC?

The questions posed in research studies, school textbooks, teacher manuals, and by teachers generally, are invariably inauthentic. They are questions that are only allowed in schools and other places where interrogation is acceptable. Dillon (1988) suggested that an essential element of an authentic question is that the questioner does not know the answer to the question posed. Imagine the response outside of school if one were to pose a question and correct the respondent's reply. For instance, ask someone directions and then evaluate their reply.

Teacher (at a gas station): "Where is the nearest fast food restaurant?"

Respondent: "Go two blocks south (pointing), hang a left, and two lights down you'll find a hamburger joint.

Teacher: "You're right. Good thinking." (Or "Wrong! There is one north, only three blocks from here.")

Outside of schools the use of the traditional Question-Response-Evaluation interaction results in some odd situations. Outside of school we expect questions to be authentic. We expect that the person asking the question does not know the answer and is interested in the information requested. However, in schools, and in school-based studies of questions and comprehension, including studies that attempt to train students to generate questions (Palincsar & Brown, 1984), authentic questions about text rarely occur.

Most of the questions posed by teachers are known-answer questions. In fact, authentic questions asked by students of teachers are truly rare, at least in instructional settings. Even procedures designed to facilitate comprehension through the joint reconstruction of the story and to make explicit the causal relationships among the states and events of stories lead to the "known," or standard, narrative structure. Such routines assume that stories have but one allowable structure and set of relationships between characters, settings, and incidents. However, Holland (1975) illustrated the difficulties with such assumptions.

It seems impossible to prepare authentic questions for a teachers' manual, because such questions only arise in the course of readers' interactions with texts and the ideas generated therein. Nonetheless, if textbook developers wish to attempt to influence the shape of the interaction after reading, then offering questions to teachers that suggest

curiosity may be more useful. For instance, one might provide postreading prompts similar to this: "As I was reading, I
found myself thinking that Katy [story character] reminded
me of a student I had several years ago. Did she remind you
of anyone?" Or, "What I found difficult to imagine was how
slowly the digging must have been [after text segment on
construction of the Panama Canal]." In other words, these
suggestions might lead students to make predictions, respond to character emotions or behaviors, or express curiosity about possible alternative actions, and so on.

Perhaps we would benefit from considering the structure of
conversations adults have with each other concerning text
that both have read (whether books, editorials, or essays). In
such situations, adults rarely interrogate each other along
the lines of the questioning found in classrooms but, rather,
they open with a question about personal response (e.g.,
"What did you think of. . . ?"), and continue with observation and evaluations and offer authentic questions (e.g., "Did
you get the part where she tried to cover up the accident?").
Adults in such situations seem to share responses and interpretation of texts rather than engage in any sort of mutual
interrogation. This is in stark contrast to the ritual of question-
asking that is carried out in school—a ritual that Bereiter
(1986) likened more to a game than any sort of authentic
lesson on understanding text.

But, considering the function and control over schooling,
can we have authentic questions and serve the accountability
function? Is it possible to move away from the ritualistic
known-answer routines that dominate classrooms? We think
it is, although the measurement of learning will, most likely,
become more time consuming. Rather than simply accepting
a listing out of the information located or remembered from
the text, we can imagine "exposition," where pupils demonstrate both deeper and broader understandings. Unfortunately, this type of evaluation will undoubtedly require not
only massive shifts in conventional wisdom about comprehension, but also changes in thinking about the nature of
schooling and learning (Tharp & Gallimore, 1989). We should
not expect that textbook developers will lead the way. Textbooks and accompanying teacher manuals are developed for
the current marketplace, not for some vision of the future
marketplace. It seems most probable that the research com-

munity will have to lead the way and this will require substantial rethinking, not only of the role of questions, but of virtually all aspects of teaching, learning, curriculum, and evaluation.

CONCLUSION

We set out to simply raise some questions about questions in texts and teaching. We have argued that conventional wisdom has led the research community to a somewhat casual acceptance of the use of questions as measures of comprehension. We offer no easy solution to the current situation but would argue that the time has come for a serious reconsideration of what we mean by learning, understanding, and comprehension. Such a reconsideration will necessarily lead to an examination of the conventional wisdom about the role that questions might play in the future design of research, curriculum, and textbooks.

REFERENCES

Allington, R. L. (1983). A commentary on Nicholson's critique of Thorndike's: Reading as reasoning—A study in paragraph reading. In L. Gentile, M. Kamil, & J. Blanchard (Eds.), *Reading research revisited* (pp. 229–234) Columbus: Merrill.

Allington, R. L., & Strange, M. (1979). Remembering is not necessarily understanding in the content areas. *Reading Horizons, 20,* 60–64.

Alvermann, D. E., & Hayes, D. A. (1989). Classroom discussion of content area reading assignments: An intervention study. *Reading Research Quarterly, 24,* 305–335.

Andre, T. (1987). Questions and learning from reading. *Questioning Exchange, 1,* 47–86.

Applebee, A. N., Langer, J. A., & Mullis, I. V. S. (1988). *Who reads best? Factors related to reading achievement in grades 3, 7, and 11.* Princeton, NJ: Educational Testing Service.

Armbruster, B. B., Anderson, T. H., Bruning, R. H., & Meyer, L. A. (1984). *What did you mean by that question?: A taxonomy of American history questions* (Tech. Rep. No. 308). Champaign, IL: Center for the Study of Reading.

Au, K. H.-P., & Kawakami, A. J. (1984). Vygotskyian perspectives on the discussion processes in small-group reading lessons. In P. L. Peterson, L. C. Wilkinson, & M. Hallinan (Eds.), *The social context of instruction: Group organization and group processes* (pp. 209–225). Orlando, FL: Academic.

Bereiter, C. (1986). The reading comprehension lesson: A commentary on Heaps' ethnomethodological analysis. *Curriculum Inquiry, 21,* 66–72.

Cole, M., & Griffin, P. (1986). A sociohistorical approach to remediation. In S. de Castell, A. Luke, & K. Egan (Eds.), *Literacy, society and schooling: A reader* (pp. 110–131). New York: Cambridge University Press.

Collins, J. (1987). Using cohesion analysis to understand access to knowledge. In D. Bloome (Ed.), *Literacy and schooling* (pp. 67–95). Norwood, NJ: Ablex.

Cronbach, L. (1955). The text in use. In L. Cronbach (Ed.), *Text materials in modern education* (pp. 188–216). Urbana, IL: University of Illinois Press.

Cuban, L. (1984). *How teachers taught, 1890–1980.* New York: Longmans.

Davey, B. (1988). How do classroom teachers use their textbooks? *Journal of Reading, 31,* 340–345.

Dillon, J. T. (1982). The effect of questions in education and other enterprises. *Journal of Curriculum Studies, 14,* 127–152.

Dillon, J. T. (1988). *Questioning and teaching: A manual of practice.* New York: Teachers College Press.

Durkin, D. (1984). Is there a match between what elementary teachers do and what basal reader manuals recommend? *Reading Teacher, 37,* 734–744.

Farrar, M. T. (1986). Teacher questions: The complexity of the cognitively simple. *Instructional Science, 15,* 89–107.

Gall, M. D. (1984). Synthesis of research on teachers' questioning. *Educational Leadership, 42,* 40–47.

Gall, M. D., Ward, B. A., Berliner, D. C., Cahen, L. S., Winne, P. H., Esashoff, J. D., & Stanton, G. C. (1978). Effects of questioning techniques and recitation on student learning. *American Educational Research Journal, 15,* 175–199.

Gambrell, L. (1984). How much time do children spend reading during teacher-directed reading instruction? In J. Niles & L. Harris (Eds.), *Changing perspectives on research in reading/language processing and instruction* (pp. 135–141). Rochester: National Reading Conference.

Goodlad, J. (1984). *A place called school.* New York: McGraw-Hill.

Goodman, K. S., Shannon, P., Freeman, Y. S., & Murphy, S. (1988). *Report card on basal readers.* Katonah, NY: Richard C. Owen.

Guszak, F. (1967). Teacher questioning and reading. *Reading Teacher, 21,* 227–234.

Hall-Quest, A. L. (1920). *The textbook: How to use and judge it.* New York: Macmillan.

Hamaker, C. (1986). The effects of adjunct questions on prose learning. *Review of Educational Research, 56,* 212–242.

Hamaker, C. (1989). Adjunct questions. In T. Husen & T. N. Postlethwaite (Eds.), *International encyclopedia of education: Research and studies, Suppl. Vol. I.* Oxford: Pergamon.

Hansen, J. (1987). *When writers read.* Portsmouth, NH: Heinemann.

Heath, S. B. (1982). Questioning at home and at school: A comparative study. In G. Spindler (Ed.), *Doing the ethnography of schooling* (pp. 105–131). New York: Holt, Rinehart & Winston.

Lalik, R., & Pecic, K. (1984). Teachers' differential selection and use of basal reader questions. In J. A. Niles & L. A. Harris (Eds.), *Changing perspec-*

tives on research in reading/language processing and instruction (pp. 199–206). Rochester, NY: National Reading Conference.

Holland, N. (1975). *Five readers reading.* New Haven, CT: Yale University Press.

Langer, J. A. (1986). *Children reading and writing.* Norwood, NJ: Ablex.

Langer, J. A., & Allington, R. L. (1992). Writing and reading curriculum. In P. Jackson (Ed.), *Handbook of curriculum research.* New York: Macmillan.

Lindfors, J. W. (1987). *Children's language and learning* (2nd ed.). Englewood Cliffs, NJ: Prentice-Hall.

O'Flahavan, J. F., Hartmann, D. K., & Pearson, P. D. (1988). Teacher questioning and feedback practices: A twenty-year retrospective. In J. E. Readence & R. S. Baldwin (Eds.), *Dialogues in literacy research* (pp. 183–208). Chicago: National Reading Conference.

Palincsar, A. S., & Brown, A. L. (1984). Reciprocal teaching of comprehension-fostering and monitoring activities. *Cognition and Instruction, 1,* 117–175.

Pearson, P. D. (1984). Asking questions about stories. In A. J. Harris & E. R. Sipay (Eds.), *Readings on reading instruction* (pp. 274–283). New York: Longmans.

Redfield, D. L., & Rousseau, E. W. (1981). A meta-analysis of experimental research on teacher questioning behavior. *Review of Educational Research, 51,* 237–245.

Rosenshine, B. V. (1980). Skill hierarchies in reading comprehension. In R. J. Spiro, B. C. Bruce, & W. F. Brewer (Eds.), *Theoretical issues in reading comprehension* (pp. 535–554). Hillsdale, NJ: Lawrence Erlbaum Associates.

Sadow, M. W. (1982). The use of story grammar in the design of questions. *Reading Teacher, 35,* 518–522.

Samson, G. E., Strykowski, B., Weinstein, T., & Walberg, H. J. (1987). The effects of teacher questioning levels on student achievement: A quantitative synthesis. *Journal of Educational Research, 80,* 290–295.

Shake, M. C., & Allington, R. L. (1985). Where do teachers' questions come from? *Reading Teacher, 38,* 432–438.

Shannon, P. (1988). *Broken Promises: Reading instruction in twentieth-century America.* South Hadley, MA: Bergin & Garvey.

Smith, N. B. (1968). *American Reading Instruction.* Newark, DE: International Reading Association.

Spring, C., Sassenrath, J., & Ketellapper, H. (1986). Ecological validity of adjunct questions in a college biology course. *Contemporary Educational Psychology, 11,* 79–89.

Staetzel, H. (1988, April). *Teachers' use of basal manuals.* Paper presented at the meeting of the Association of American Publishers, School Division, Washington, DC.

Taylor, B., Olson, V., Prenn, M., Rybczynski, M., & Zakaluk, B. (1985). A comparison of students' ability to read for main ideas in social studies textbooks and to complete main idea worksheets. *Reading World, 24,* 10–15.

Tharp, R., & Gallimore, R. (1989). Rousing schools to life. *American Educator, 13,* 20–25.

Thorndike, E. L. (1917). Reading as reasoning: A study of mistakes in paragraph reading. *Journal of Educational Psychology, 8,* 323–332.

Tyson-Bernstein, H. (1988). *A conspiracy of good intentions: America's textbook fiasco.* Washington, DC: Council for Basic Education.

Venezky, R. L. (1986). Steps toward a modern history of American reading instruction. In E. Z. Rothkopf (Ed.), *Review of Research in Education, 13,* 129–167.

Weber, R. (1986, April). *Constraints on the questioning routine in reading instruction.* Paper presented at the annual meeting of the American Educational Research Association, San Francisco.

Wendler, D., Samuels, S. J., & Moore, V. K. (1989). Comprehension instruction of award-winning teachers, teachers with masters degrees, and other teachers. *Reading Research Quarterly, 24,* 382–401.

Wixson, K. K. (1983). Postreading question-answer interactions and children's learning from text. *Journal of Educational Psychology, 30,* 413–423.

Woodward, A. (1986). Taking teaching out of teaching and reading out of learning to read: An historical study of reading textbook teachers' guides, 1920–1980. *Book Research Quarterly, 8,* 53–73.

Questions in Elementary Science and Social Studies Textbooks

Bonnie Armbruster
University of Illinois at Urbana-Champaign

Joyce Ostertag
Benchmark School, Media, Pennsylvania

The powerful role of textbooks in the American curriculum is by now well established. "According to virtually all studies of the matter, textbooks have become the *de facto* curriculum of the public schools, as well as the *de facto* mechanism for controlling teachers" (Tyson-Bernstein, 1988, p. 11).

An important part of the curriculum offered in textbooks is questions. As Gall (1970) observed, "It is a truism that questions play an important role in teaching" (p. 707). Questions serve two main functions: One function is instructional—to promote learning. Questions are included in teachers' manuals before, during, and after lessons in order to motivate students, set purposes for reading, focus attention, promote and assess comprehension, and foster skill development. Questions appear in the student text and workbooks for many of the same reasons. The second function of questions is to assess learning. In this capacity, questions are the very substance of tests covering chapters and units included in textbook materials.

Questions are important and pervasive in the *de facto* curriculum of textbooks. They embody, in a very real sense, the instructional philosophy of the publishers. They reflect the content and skills deemed important and worthy of instructional time and attention. To administrators, teachers, parents, and students, questions deliver a message about educational goals and priorities.

Therefore, it is important to know the nature of questions in commercially published materials. However, we are not aware of any recent research (within the last 15 years) on questions in materials other than basal readers. Therefore, this study investigates the characteristics of the questions asked in content area materials. Specifically, the study addresses the issues of how many and what kind of questions—both instructional and assessment—appear in recent fourth- and fifth-grade science and social studies textbooks and teachers' manuals. The intent examines the pattern of questioning with respect to research recommendations on questioning and the implicit educational philosophy.

METHOD

Materials

The materials were fourth- and fifth-grade science and social studies texts (pupils' and teachers' editions) of three major publishers. We selected materials at Grades 4 and 5 because it is at these levels that students are beginning to learn to "read to learn"; therefore, content area textbooks play an especially important instructional role. We selected textbooks from three companies who publish both science and social studies programs: Harcourt Brace Javanovich, Scott, Foresman, and Silver Burdett. These programs command a respectable portion of the market and are representative of commercially published materials. When we began the study, we used the most recent versions of the textbooks available to us. The specific textbooks included in the study are listed in Table 3.1. Because we were interested in general trends rather than specific publisher differences, we did not include publishers as a factor in our analysis.

Procedure

Development of a Question Classification System. Researchers have developed many systems for classifying questions, but the most commonly used systems are based

TABLE 3.1

Textbooks Used in Analysis

Fourth Grade

Social Studies

States and Regions. Orlando, FL: Harcourt Brace Jovanovich Publishing Co., 1985.

Regions of Our Country and Our World. Glenview, IL: Scott, Foresman Publishing Co., 1983.

States and Regions. Morristown, NJ: Silver Burdett Co., 1986.

Science

HBJ Science. Orlando, FL: Harcourt Brace Jovanovich Publishing Co., 1985.

Scott, Foresman Science. Glenview, IL: Scott, Foresman Publishing Co., 1984.

Silver Burdett Science. Morristown, NJ: Silver Burdett Co., 1986.

Fifth Grade

Social Studies

The United States: Its History and Neighbors. Orlando, FL: Harcourt Brace Jovanovich Publishing Co., 1985.

America Past and Present. Glenview, IL: Scott, Foresman Publishing Co., 1983.

The United States and its Neighbors. Morristown, NJ: Silver Burdett Co., 1986.

Science

HBJ Science. Orlando, FL: Harcourt Brace Jovanovich Publishing Co., 1985.

Scott, Foresman Science. Glenview, IL: Scott, Foresman Publishing Co., 1984.

Silver Burdett Science. Morristown, NJ: Silver Burdett Co., 1985.

---

on the type of cognitive process presumed to be required to answer the question (Gall, 1970, 1984). Bloom's taxonomy of educational objectives for the cognitive domain (Bloom, Engelhart, Furst, Hill, & Krathwohl, 1956) has undoubtedly been the most influential so far in research on questioning. This six-level hierarchical system assumes a continuum of cognitive demands, ranging from relatively simple to more complex. The six levels are explained briefly here:

1. *Knowledge* refers to the ability to recall information, such as memorize formulas or dates.
2. *Comprehension* involves translating, interpreting, or extrapolating information in order to show understanding; it also refers to the ability to use the in-

formation. Examples of comprehension include explaining a diagram, interpreting a poem, or predicting what might happen next in a story.

3. *Application* entails using knowledge and principles to solve problems. Using Bloom's taxonomy to design classroom objectives or using knowledge of math relationships to solve word problems are examples of application.

4. *Analysis* involves breaking down complex information into its component parts in order to understand the underlying structure and relationships. Examples of analysis are identifying the parts of a simple story or contrasting authors' styles.

5. *Synthesis* refers to creating something new, such as writing a composition or designing an experiment.

6. *Evaluation* entails judging something against an internal or external criterion or standard; for example, evaluating a proposed solution to a problem or evaluating a summary for accuracy and completeness.

Another popular taxonomy influenced by Bloom's taxonomy is that of Smith and Barrett (1979), which was designed specifically for reading comprehension. The Smith and Barrett taxonomy has four major categories:

1. *Literal recognition or recall* involves recognition and recall of information stated explicitly in text. Examples of this category are recognizing or recalling details, main ideas, sequence, comparisons, cause and effect, and character traits.

2. *Inference* refers to synthesizing text content with personal knowledge, intuition, and imagination to form conjectures or hypotheses. This category includes inferring details, main ideas, sequence, comparisons, cause and effect, and character traits, as well as predicting outcomes and making inferences about figurative language.

3. *Evaluation* involves forming judgments by making comparisons with external or internal criteria. Examples of evaluation are judgments of reality or fantasy, fact or opinion, adequacy or validity, appropriateness, worth, desirability, or acceptability.

4. *Appreciation* concerns awareness of the literary techniques, forms, styles, and structures used by authors
   to stimulate emotional responses in readers. Appreciation includes emotional response to a plot or theme,
   identification with characters and incidents, reactions to the author's use of language, and imagery.

In our opinion, one interesting aspect of the Smith and
Barrett taxonomy is the subdivision of categories according
to the specific type of information targeted by the question
(e.g., recognizing and recalling main ideas, inferring cause
and effect relationships, identification with characters and
incidents).

A third taxonomy, popular in the last decade, is Pearson
and Johnson's (1978) taxonomy of question–answer relationships. This taxonomy is based on recent theories of reading,
which stress that reading is not simply a text-based activity,
but an interactive process in which meaning evolves from an
interaction of reader with text. The three categories of the
Pearson and Johnson taxonomy are identified by the data
source that must be used by the reader to answer the
question:

1. *Textually explicit.* Both question and answer are
   derivable from the text and the relationship between
   them is explicitly cued by the language of the text.
2. *Textually implicit.* Both question and answer are
   derivable from the text, but the answer is not explicitly cued by the language of the text. In other words,
   the answer must be inferred from the text.
3. *Scriptally implicit.* The question is derivable from
   the text, but the answer depends on the reader's
   background knowledge or "script."

Table 3.2 represents our best guess about how the three
taxonomies compare with each other.

We were not totally satisfied with any of these three
classification systems. Although Pearson and Johnson's taxonomy is most responsive to current reading theory, we
found that the three categories, particularly the textually
implicit category, were too broad for our purposes. Bloom's
and Smith and Barrett's taxonomies came closer to reflecting

TABLE 3.2
A Comparison of Three Question Taxonomies

Bloom et al. (1956)	Smith & Barrett (1979)	Pearson & Johnson (1978)
Knowledge	Literal recognition or recall	Textually explicit
Comprehension	Inference	Textually implicit
Application		
Analysis		
Synthesis		Scriptally implicit
Evaluation	Evaluation	
	Appreciation	

the variety of cognitive demands that we thought were required by different types of questions. But these taxonomies also had their weaknesses. Neither taxonomy recognizes that reading involves an interaction of reader and text and the resulting need to consider question–answer relationships. We found Bloom's taxonomy difficult to use; perhaps because it is a taxonomy of educational objectives rather than questions per se, we were often puzzled about how to classify particular questions. Smith and Barrett's taxonomy was somewhat easier to use, but it appeared to be more appropriate for narrative than for expository text. For example, examples such as inferring character traits and identifying with characters and incidents would not be represented in social studies and science textbooks.

We finally decided to compromise by including aspects of all three taxonomies in our own classification system. Our system includes five categories. The first category, *Type of Question,* uses a modification of Bloom's and Smith and Barrett's taxonomies in an attempt to index the type of cognitive process students would probably use to answer the question. This category includes five subcategories of questions, which are defined and illustrated in Table 3.3.

The second category, *Source of Answer,* is included in response to Pearson and Johnson's concern about the need to consider question–answer relationships. We determined four possible sources of answers for textbook questions: the prose itself, graphic aids, activities or demonstrations, and prior knowledge. These sources are defined and exemplified in Table 3.4. In coding questions in this category, we tried to determine the single most likely source of the answer, even

TABLE 3.3
Definitions and Examples of "Type of Question" Dimension

Type 1. Answering a Type 1 question involves little or no inferencing. The answer is either (a) explicitly stated in the text within a single sentence, or (b) assumed to be an intact part of memory (i.e., stored in exactly the required form). This level is similar to the "knowledge" level of Bloom's taxonomy, the "literal recognition and recall" level of Smith and Barrett's taxonomy, and the "textually explicit" level of the Pearson-Johnson taxonomy.

Examples: (Example 1 illustrates Point a; Example 2 illustrates Point b)

1. The frontier was the imaginary dividing line between (a) *the North and South* (b) *California gold mining camps* (c) *settled and unsettled land.* (*America Past and Present,* Teacher's Edition, 1983, p. 123)

(The text says: "The frontier was the imaginary dividing line between settled and unsettled land." *America Past and Present,* 1983, p. 194)

2. What is this a statue of? (*The United States: Its History and Neighbors,* 1985, p. 338)

(There is an uncaptioned photograph of a statue of Abraham Lincoln. Students either know the answer or not; there is no possibility of inferring a correct answer.)

Type 2. Answering a Type 2 question involves some inferencing. The answer is either (a) in the text but must be inferred across sentences or paragraphs, or (b) assumed to be part of prior knowledge, but probably not stored in exactly the required form. (This level is similar to the "comprehension" level of Bloom's taxonomy, the "inferential" level of Smith and Barrett's taxonomy, and the "textually implicit" level of the Pearson-Johnson taxonomy.)

Examples: (Example 1 illustrates Point a; Example 2 illustrates Point b)

1. How did cities grow upward and outward?
(*America Past and Present,* 1983, p. 318)

(This example requires students to pull together information over several pages of text.)

2. What is going on in the picture? (*The United States: Its History and Neighbors,* 1985, p. 358)

(This example requires students to make an inference from an uncaptioned picture of: soldiers fighting, a cannon, and a flag.)

Type 3. Answering a Type 3 question involves applying information from the text or prior knowledge to a novel situation. (This level is similar to the "application" level of Bloom's taxonomy and is included in the "inferential" level of Smith and Barrett's taxonomy and the "textually implicit" level of the Pearson-Johnson taxonomy.)

(continued)

TABLE 3.3 *(Continued)*

Examples:

1. Did Andrew Carnegie's company provide goods or services?
(*The United States: Its History and Neighbors,* Teacher's Edition, 1985, p. 408)

(This question requires students to apply new knowledge about the distinction between goods and services to recently read information about Andrew Carnegie.)

2. What simple machines are found in this compound machine?
(*Silver Burdett Science,* Teacher's Edition, Grade 4, 1985, p. 66.)

(This question requires students to find examples of the simple machines they have read about in a simple line drawing of a wheelbarrow.)

Type 4. Answering a Type 4 question involves putting together information in order to make predictions, generate hypotheses, and form analogies. (This level is included in the "comprehension" levels in Bloom's taxonomy, the "inferential" level of Smith and Barrett's taxonomy, and the "scriptally implicit" level of the Pearson-Johnson taxonomy.)

Examples:

1. Imagine the United States with no Mississippi River. How would the country be different? What towns might be different? How might people's lives be different?
(*Regions of Our Country and Our World,* 1983, p. 315)

2. What would happen if the lens in your eye was not able to change its shape?
(*Scott, Foresman Science,* Grade 5, 1984, p. 279)

(These two questions require students to generate hypotheses or make predictions based on information they have just read.)

3. Have the students compare a bus system with the systems in the body.
(*Silver Burdett Science,* Teacher's Edition, 1985, p. 273)

(These questions require students to form an analogy between information they have just read and prior knowledge.)

Type 5. Answering a Type 5 question involves making value judgments about events or situations based on information presented in the text and internal criteria. (This level is similar to the "evaluation" levels in Bloom's, and Smith and Barrett's taxonomies, and is included in the "scriptally implicit" level of the Pearson-Johnson taxonomy.)

Examples:

1. If you were a farmer, which would you prefer to use—horses or a tractor? Why?
(*Regions of Our Country and the World,* Teacher's Edition, 1983, p. 397)

2. Where would you rather live—in a cold, dry place or in a cold, wet place? Why?
(*States and Regions,* 1985, p. 258)

TABLE 3.4

Definitions and Examples of Questions in "Source of Answer" Dimension

Prose. The answer is primarily derivable from the prose itself.

Examples:

1. How did the coming of the first white settlers to America change the forests?
(*States and Regions*, 1986, p. 35)

The text says: "The first white settlers cut down many trees. They built their homes of wood and cleared fields for farming. They used wood as a fuel for heating their houses and for cooking. As people moved west, more trees were cut. Forests were destroyed to make farmland and to make room for highways and railroads." (*States and Regions*, 1986, p. 34)

2. The surface of a mirror is always
a. *very smooth* b. *very rough*
c. *made of silver* (*HBJ Science*, Grade 4, 1984, p. 91)

The text says: "The reflecting surface of a mirror is very smooth." (*HBJ Science*, Grade 4, p. 90)

Graphic. The answer is primarily derivable from a picture, photograph, diagram, chart, table, time line, map, or globe.

Examples:

1. Reading a Time Line. Have pupils use the time line on this page to answer the following questions . . .
(*The United States and its Neighbors*, Grade 5, 1986, p. 108)

2. (Refers to unit opening photographs) How are these animals different?
(*HBJ Science*, Teacher's Edition, Grade 4, 1985, TM1).

Activity. The answer is primarily derivable from an activity demonstrated by the teacher or completed by the students.

Examples:

1. What happened when you let a lot of water fall quickly on the sand in the same place?
(*Scott, Foresman Science*, Grade 4, 1984, p. 115).

(This question follows an activity about water as an agent of change.)

2. Which leaf is wilted?
(*HBJ Science*, Grade 5, 1985, p. 277)

(This question follows an activity comparing plants in salt and fresh water environments.)

Prior Knowledge. The answer depends primarily on what the reader already knows, rather than on information presented in the text.

Examples:

1. Ask the class to describe what can happen to metal objects when they are left outside for many weeks.
(*Scott, Foresman Science*, Grade 4, 1984, p. 117)

(This question precedes text discussing rust.)

2. Is there a river near our community?
(*The United States: Its History and Neighbors*, 1985 p. 54)

though students may have been able to use a different source
or more than one source to generate the answer. Also, "the
answer" refers to the answer given in the teacher's edition.
Where answers were missing or obviously wrong or inappropriate, we determined an appropriate answer.

The third dimension is *Target Relationship*. In including
this category, we were influenced by Smith and Barrett's
taxonomy, with its attention to the particular type of relationship (e.g., sequence, cause–effect, comparison) asked for in
the question. Table 3.5 defines and gives examples of the
subcategories of questions in the Target Relationship category.

A fourth category in our classification system is *Form of
Question*. The subcategories of Forms of Questions are
multiple-choice; true/false; matching; fill-in; short answer
(requiring an answer consisting of anything from a single
word to two sentences); essay (requiring an answer of three or
more sentences); and graphic (requiring an answer in the
form of a picture, diagram, chart, map, etc.).

Finally, we included a fifth dimension called *Question
Purpose* because we were interested in differentiating between questions that were included primarily for instructional purposes and those included primarily for assessment
purposes. Instructional questions included questions in: (a)
the teacher's edition (except tests), (b) the pupils' edition at
the ends of lessons and/or chapters, (c) activities, such as
science investigations, and (d) chapter or unit reviews. Assessment questions included items on chapter and unit tests.

Question Analysis.   First, we developed a coding sheet
on which to record information about question number and
the five categories of questions previously described (*Type of
Question, Source of Answer, Target Relationship, Form of
Question,* and *Purpose of Question*).

Next, we conducted a small pilot study to test our classification system. Both authors worked together to code the
questions from four randomly selected chapters from the
previously described textbook sample. This exercise enabled
us to reach consensus on what counted as a question and
how various representative question types should best be
coded. Then we were ready to begin the major study.

We randomly sampled two units from each textbook in our

TABLE 3.5
Definitions and Examples of Questions in "Target Relationship"
Dimension

Process. Process questions ask about a sequence of events or series of steps that are not necessarily causally connected.

Examples:

1. Describe, in sequence, the events that occur in pond succession.
(*Silver Burdett Science,* Teacher's Edition, Grade 5, 1985, p. 100)

2. Number the events below from 1 to 7 in the order that they happened.
(Seven events from the Civil War follow.)
(*America Past and Present,* Teacher's Edition, Grade 5, 1983, p. 127)

Cause-Effect. Cause-effect questions ask about a causal relationship between an antecedent and a consequent.

Examples:

1. Near the mid-ocean ridges, magma breaks through easily because the
   a. *Earth's crust is very thick there.*
   b. *Earth's plates are rigid there.*
   c. *Earth's crust is very thin there.*
   d. *crust is hot enough to melt rock.*
(*HBJ Science,* Teacher's Edition, Grade 5, 1985, p. 27)

2. Why did the government keep troops in the South for several years after the Civil War?
(*America Past and Present,* Teacher's Edition, 1983, p. 161)

Definition. Definition questions ask for a definition of a concept.

Examples:

1. What is refraction?
(*Scott, Foresman Science,* Grade 5, 1984, p. 275)

2. Capital is (a) *saved up wealth,* (b) *natural resources.*
(*The United States and its Neighbors,* 1986, p. 218)

Property. Property questions ask about properties or characteristics of objects or events.

Examples:

1. When it hatches, a salmon is usually
   a. *about 2 meters long.*
   b. *about 2 centimeters long.*
   c. *about 20 centimeters long.*
   d. *about ½ meter long.*
(*HBJ Science,* Teacher's Edition, 1985, p. 45P)

2. Describe a cool, fairly dry climate.
(*Regions of Our Country and Our World,* 1983, p. 263)

(continued)

TABLE 3.5 *(Continued)*

Example. Example questions ask for one or more examples of a concept.

Examples:

1. Name a bird that cannot fly.
(*Silver Burdett Science,* Teacher's Edition, Grade 5, p. 67)

2. What were some of the problems the homesteaders faced?
(*The United States: Its History and Neighbors,* 1985, p. 430)

Identity. Identity questions ask for the name of a person, object, event, or concept described in the question.

Examples:

1. It is a cold-blooded vertebrate. Its body is covered with scales. It can change color for protection. What is it?
(*Silver Burdett Science,* Grade 5, 1985, p. 78)

2. What is the highest mountain in the world?
(*States and Regions,* 1986, p. 371)

Compare/Contrast. Compare/contrast questions ask for similarities and/or differences between two or more concepts or events.

Examples:

1. Compare conduction and convection.
(*Silver Burdett Science,* Grade 4, 1985, p. 76)

2. The Quechuas must depend on themselves to meet their needs. How is their life in the Andes different from life in the city?
(*States and Regions,* 1986, p. 371)

No Relationship. No relationship questions do not ask for a relationship between ideas. This category includes questions that ask for only Yes/No answers, True/False questions, and questions for which it was unclear what relationship was being assessed.

Examples:

1. If you lived on Pluto or Neptune, would you be able to celebrate your birthday frequently?
(*HBJ Science,* Teacher's Edition, Grade 5, 1985, p. 102)

2. True/False Slavery continued in the northern states for many years after the Civil War.
(*America Past and Present,* 1983, p. 322)

sample. (Two units comprised between one quarter and one third of the total content of each textbook.) Then we identified and numbered each candidate question. The following types of questions were included in the analysis:

1. standard wh- and how questions;
2. "pseudoquestions" (Pearson & Johnson, 1978), that is, questions stated in the imperative rather than the

interrogative form (e.g., "Explain what the Continental Divide is.");

3. indirect or implicit questions in the teacher's edition (e.g., "Encourage students to talk about the hardships and dangers explorers would have had to face in the early 1800s").

Excluded from the analysis were questions embedded within the prose of the pupils' edition (because these are often rhetorical questions, with no apparent expectation of a response) and questions within special "skills lessons" appearing within the unit.

Both authors independently coded every question. The analysis required us to consider each question in relationship to both the instructional context (the text and the instruction recommended in the teacher's edition) and the expected answer (given in the teacher's edition). Therefore, we had to carefully read the pupils' edition as well as the teacher's edition in order to complete the analysis. After coding the questions in each chapter, we compared our results. Every discrepancy was resolved through discussion; thus, we reached 100% consensus on the final coding. In all, 7,463 questions were coded in this manner.

The data were analyzed by computer using a Statistical Package for the Social Sciences (SPSS) program, Crosstabs, which yields frequencies and percentages of questions in the various categories of our system.

In addition to investigating question characteristics, we were also interested in determining question density; we calculated question density as the number of words of text divided by the number of questions.

RESULTS AND DISCUSSION

Question Characteristics

Tables 3.6 to 3.9 present the percentages of total instructional and assessment questions in the sampled social studies and science materials for the categories of *Type of Question, Target Relationship, Source of Answer,* and *Form of Question,* respectively.

Type of Question. As Table 3.6 shows, almost half of the instructional questions and two thirds of the assessment questions are Type 1 questions—questions involving little or no inference. The next most frequent question type is Type 2 questions—questions that require students to make some degree of inference. About one half of instructional questions in social studies and between one quarter and one third of instructional questions in science are questions of this type. For both social studies and science, however, only about one quarter of the assessment questions require some degree of inference. In both content areas, Type 4, 5, and 6 questions are relatively sparse in either instruction or assessment.

The profile of question types we found differs somewhat from the findings of earlier studies on questions in commercially published materials. Davis and Hunkins (1965) analyzed all questions from a sample of chapters from three fifth-grade social studies textbooks, using Bloom's taxonomy. They concluded that about 87% of the questions required knowledge of specifics, whereas only about 9% required comprehension. Trachtenberg (1974), again using Bloom's taxonomy, analyzed all the study questions, exercises, activities, and test items in nine sets of commercially published world history materials. Of the almost 62,000 items analyzed, an average of about 63% were "knowledge" and about 36% were "comprehension" items, with a negli-

TABLE 3.6
Distribution of Questions by Type

Content Area	Question Purpose	Type of Question				
		Type 1	Type 2	Type 3	Type 4	Type 5
Social Studies	Instructional (n = 3,529)	45.6%	45.0%	3.7%	4.0%	1.7%
	Assessment (n = 866)	68.7%	28.6%	2.5%	0.0%	0.1%
Science	Instructional (n = 2,609)	46.0%	28.9%	16.4%	8.4%	0.3%
	Assessment (n = 459)	66.7%	26.4%	6.8%	0.2%	0.0%

gible number of items representing the higher cognitive levels.

Unfortunately, it is very difficult to compare results across studies because of the variety of terms used to describe different levels of questions in different research studies. As Carrier and Fautsch-Patridge (1981) stated, "The diversity of names and categories used to describe different levels of questions is symptomatic of an underlying confusion which makes interstudy comparisons difficult" (p. 366). However, assuming that our Type 1 and Type 2 categories are similar to Bloom's knowledge and comprehension levels, respectively, our results show a profile quite different from Davis and Hunkin's and somewhat different from Trachtenberg's. At least for instructional questions, we found fewer Type 1 questions, more Type 2 questions, and more questions in the other categories. For assessment questions, however, our results look more similar to Trachtenberg's findings.

How might the profile of question types we found affect student learning? Two lines of research bear on the answer to this question: (a) research on the effect of having students answer questions inserted in textbook passages (so called "adjunct questions"); and (b) research on the effect of teacher questions on learning.

In his meta-analysis of research on adjunct questions, Hamaker (1986) concluded that "higher order questions may have a somewhat broader general facilitative effect than factual adjunct questions" (p. 237). Andre (1987), in his extensive review of the adjunct question literature, concluded that "higher level adjunct questions facilitate the learning of factual information from text and increase the amount of attention readers devote to processing text" (p. 81). Thus, these two recent, major reviews of adjunct questions tend to give the nod to higher order questions.

Another conclusion derived from research on adjunct questions in that such questions have a so-called "forward effect" (Rickards, 1979). That is, students form expectations based on the type of question they receive, and these expectations affect learning from reading subsequent material. In other words, students' interactions with questions directly influence future learning outcomes. The implication is that higher order questions should be asked if the goal of instruction is to promote higher order processing of the text.

The results of research on teacher questions is less straight-forward. Gall (1984) pointed out the discrepancies in three major reviews of research on teacher questioning. In a review of correlational studies, Rosenshine (1976) concluded that students learn best when teacher questions "tend to be narrow [i.e., factual], pupils are expected to know rather than guess [the] answer, and the teacher immediately reinforces an answer as right or wrong" (p. 365). In a review of experimental studies, Winne (1979) concluded that "whether teachers use predominantly higher cognitive questions or predominantly fact questions makes little difference in student achievement" (p. 13). Finally, Redfield and Rousseau's (1981) meta-analysis of experimental studies led them to the conclusion that "predominant use of higher level questions during instruction has a positive effect on student achievement" (p. 241).

In pondering the differences among the student populations sampled in the studies reviewed by Rosenshine, Winne, and Redfield and Rousseau, Gall (1984) hypothesized the following reconciliation of the apparently conflicting conclusions: "(1) emphasis on fact questions is more effective for promoting young disadvantaged children's achievement, which primarily involves mastery of basic skills; and (2) Emphasis on higher cognitive questions is more effective for students of average and high ability, especially as they enter high school, where more independent thinking is required" (p. 41).

Other research on teacher questions indicates that students' responses to teachers' questions tend to be at about the same level of cognitive complexity as the teachers' questions. Thus, asking higher order questions seems to encourage students to engage in higher levels of cognitive processing (Dillon, 1982).

In summary, the research on text and teacher questions tends to support the use of higher level questions in instruction. Questions requiring processing at a higher cognitive level appear to promote learning of questioned material as well as to shape student processing of subsequent material. As Wixson (1983) stated, "What you ask about is what children learn" (p. 287).

To return to the question of how the profile of question types we found might affect student learning, we offer the following observations: Because we found more Type 1 (factual) questions than any other kind, it appears that the questions in the materials we analyzed do not conform to the research-based recommendations about higher level questions. However, this seeming indictment needs some qualification.

First the picture is not as bleak as we thought it might be. We were encouraged by the higher proportion of Type 2 questions than we had been expecting based on previous research.

Second, we were impressed by the relatively high degree of cognitive processing required by some of the Type 2 questions. Our Type 2 category includes questions that require rather complex inferences, such as pulling together information from several locations in the text to answer a "main idea" question. Indeed, we felt that some Type 2 questions require higher levels of cognitive processing than did some Type 3 to Type 5 questions. For example, the Type 5 question, "If you were a farmer, which would you prefer to use—horses or a tractor?" "Why?" may well promote less sophisticated thinking than the Type 2 question, "How do the juices given off by the mouth, stomach, and small intestine help in digestion?" (given that the information required to answer the question comes from several different sections). (Our observation that a hierarchy of cognitive processing does not exist in our classification system led us to label our categories *Types* rather than *Levels*.)

Third, the research does not suggest what an appropriate distribution of questions should be. Redfield and Rousseau (1981) concluded that achievement is facilitated by a predominant use of higher level questions during instruction, but they do not define "predominant." Certainly no one suggests that all questions should be high level. Indeed, the use of factual questions can be defended on the grounds that students need to know certain basic information before they can engage in higher order thinking.

A fourth qualification has to do with the measure of relative frequencies of questions in the different categories. The occurrence of relatively fewer high-level than low-level questions may simply be an artifact of the population of possible items to draw from. That is, for a given unit of text, there are probably fewer potential higher level than lower level questions. For example, in a particular lesson, there may be hundreds of possibilities for "factual" items, but only one or two possibilities for good "main idea" items. Also, for some texts, questions calling for applications, predictions, hypotheses, or evaluations may simply be inappropriate. For example, there may be no obvious opportunity for an application question about the settlement of Rhode Island or an evaluation question about symbiosis. Therefore, the materials may contain a reasonable *absolute* number of Type 2 to Type 5 questions; it may be only that the number looks small *relative* to the high number of Type 1 questions.

A fifth and final qualification relates to the goals of instruction in fourth- and fifth-grade science and social studies. A predominant use of higher order questions is appropriate if the goal of instruction is to promote higher order thinking skills. But if the goal is to have students learn facts and understand concepts and principles, then the type of questions in the materials we analyzed may well be quite appropriate. Of course, it is not easy to determine what the implicit goals of instruction *are*, much less what they *should be*.

The preceding points notwithstanding, we believe that too high a proportion of the questions in these science and social studies materials are factual questions, requiring little or no inference from single text sentences. When half of the questions asked by the teacher or textbook and two thirds of the test questions ask for facts, students are getting a clear message about educational priorities. Furthermore, they are learning to engage in minimal cognitive processing and to rely on copying or rote memorization.

Target Relationships. Table 3.7 shows the relative frequency of the Target Relationships asked in questions. The most frequent instructional questions in both social studies and science are cause–effect questions. This result seems reasonable; after all, explanations of causality are the heart of science and social studies. The prevalence of cause–effect questions is consistent with a finding in a previous study of history questions (Armbruster, Anderson, Bruning, & Meyer, 1984), where explanation questions predominated. The next most frequent target relationships asked in instructional questions are identity (asking for the name of a described

TABLE 3.7

Distribution of Questions by Target Relationships

| | | | | | | | *Target Relationship* | | |
Content Area	Question Purpose	Process	Cause/ Effect	Definition	Property	Example	Identity	Compare Contrast	None
Social Studies	Instructional (*n* = 3,529)	1.0%	27.9%	11.6%	5.7%	18.9%	22.4%	8.1%	4.2%
	Assessment (*n* = 866)	0.8%	14.2%	29.7%	4.8%	9.1%	35.0%	3.0%	3.3%
Science	Instructional (*n* = 2,609)	3.4%	26.0%	10.3%	10.2%	13.3%	17.4%	11.0%	8.4%
	Assessment (*n* = 459)	0.7%	20.0%	23.7%	13.3%	9.8%	26.6%	3.7%	2.2%

concept or object) and example (asking for examples of a concept).

For assessment questions, the profile is different. About half of the total questions are identity and definition questions. These two question types are closely related: *Identity questions* define or describe a concept or object and ask for a name, whereas *definition questions* provide the name of a concept or object and ask for a definition. In other words, this finding shows that students are being held accountable largely for names and definitions. Knowledge of cause–effect relationships receives lower priority in assessment than in instruction.

Source of Answer. The relative frequency of Source of Answer is shown in Table 3.8. It is not surprising that three quarters of instructional questions in science require text-based answers. Graphics are the second greatest source of instructional questions in social studies but the least source in science instruction. Again, it is not surprising that many questions in social studies refer to maps, charts, and tables. The fact that a greater proportion of instructional questions in science are based on activities is also not surprising, because science instruction typically includes many "hands-on" activities or demonstrations. The finding that science instruction includes more prior knowledge items than social studies is consistent with the finding that science materials

TABLE 3.8
Distribution of Questions by Source of Answer

Content Area	Question Purpose	Source of Answer			
		Text	Graphic	Activity	Prior Knowledge
Social Studies	Instructional (n = 3,529)	76.7%	13.8%	0.5%	8.9%
	Assessment (n = 866)	94.1%	4.8%	0.0%	1.0%
Science	Instructional (n = 2,609)	55.5%	10.0%	17.9%	16.6%
	Assessment (n = 459)	92.4%	6.3%	0.2%	1.1%

have more Type 4 questions (see Table 3.3). Questions that ask for predictions, hypotheses, and analogies obviously require the reader to draw on prior knowledge.

The relative frequency of Source of Answer questions is different for assessment, however. In both content areas, over 90% of the questions are based on information in the text, a finding that seems reasonable to us.

Form of Question. Table 3.9 shows the relative frequency of Form of Question. About five-sixths of instructional questions are short-answer questions. This is hardly surprising, because it is difficult for teachers to ask questions orally in any other form. For assessment questions, about one half are multiple choice; matching is the second most popular form of question. True–false, fill-in, and short answer questions round out the profile of assessment questions. This situation is probably attributable to (a) the belief that teachers prefer easily scorable, objective tests; and (b) the pervasive influence of standardized tests and standardized test formats.

The commercially published materials offer very few opportunities for students to synthesize and integrate extended information in an essay. We think this is unfortunate, considering the current emphasis on writing and the relationship between reading and writing (see, e.g., Squire, 1983).

Question Density

Density of questions was calculated by dividing total number of words of text by total number of instructional and assessment questions. The results are shown in Table 3.10.

To have an instructional question for about every 30 words of text seems excessive to us. First, it ensures that many of the questions will be factual. Second, the instructional question dictates frequent interruptions of reading. Frequent interruptions make it difficult for students to keep track of the main ideas, to form a coherent interpretation of the information, and to engage in higher order cognition. Overly frequent questioning, in combination with a high proportion of Type 1 questions, may encourage students to be locaters of information rather than learners of content.

It may not be the publishers' intent that teachers ask all the

TABLE 3.9

Distribution of Questions by Form

Content Area	Question Purpose	Form of Question						
		Multiple Choice	True/ False	Matching	Fill-In	Short Answer	Essay	Graphic
Social Studies	Instructional (n = 3,529)	2.9%	4.3%	5.6%	0.7%	84.2%	1.9%	0.4%
	Assessment (n = 866)	49.7%	9.2%	16.4%	9.6%	10.2%	3.3%	1.6%
Science	Instructional (n = 2,609)	6.6%	0.9%	5.4%	2.4%	82.7%	0.7%	1.3%
	Assessment (n = 459)	48.8%	11.3%	15.7%	10.7%	10.7%	1.7%	1.1%

TABLE 3.10
Question Density: Mean Number of Words of Text Per Question

Content Area	Question Purpose	
	Instructional	Assessment
Social Studies	36.4	148.4
Science	26.5	144.7

questions in the teacher's edition, but rather to ask questions selectively as time permits. Indeed, given the large number of questions, teachers probably would not have time to ask all of them. Yet no guidelines for question priorities are offered in the teacher's editions; the lack of a differentiated list of questions gives the impression that all of the questions are equal in value.

CONCLUDING COMMENTS AND RECOMMENDATIONS

Many of the problems with questions in commercially published materials exist because there is not yet a science of questioning. An important part of creating a science of questioning will involve the development of alternative methods of assessment. There is currently a serious discrepancy between what we know about learning from text and how we measure that learning. Fortunately, this urgent problem is beginning to be addressed (see, e.g., Valencia & Pearson, 1986).

One probable outcome of work on new methods of assessment is the development of new taxonomies, or at least typologies, of questions. The available taxonomies (e.g., Bloom's, Barrett's, and Pearson and Johnson's) seem to fall short of capturing all the important dimensions of questions as recognized by current cognitive psychology. We feel that our own effort at a multidimensional taxonomy is an improvement, but our effort, too, has its weaknesses. For example, our Type 2 category (as well as Bloom's comprehension level, Smith and Barrett's inferential level, and Pearson and Johnson's text-implicit category) is too broad to reflect important differences in cognitive processing required of different questions. We believe a question taxonomy should reflect finer distinctions in the requisite cognitive processing.

Of course, hand in hand with the development of new assessment methods, there must be further research on issues such as the optimal type, number, and sequencing of questions to use in furthering various desired educational outcomes.

However, as we await the development of a science of questioning, we offer the following recommendations to publishers of science and social studies materials and to the teachers who use them.

1. Because we think commercially published materials contain far too many questions, we recommend reducing the number of questions by weeding out those that do not reinforce or assess important content.

2. We believe that many of the remaining lower order (Type 1) questions should be transformed into higher order questions that get students to think rather than to copy or memorize. With very little effort, such as a paraphrase here and a request for support or evidence there, questions could tap the same basic information but demand considerably more cognitive processing. For instance, most multiple-choice (recognition) items could be restated as recall items that would involve greater cognitive processing. The question, "When a cloud forms, water vapor in the air (a) *evaporates,* (b) *condenses,* or (c) *falls to the earth*" could be restated as "Explain how clouds form." The latter question potentially requires greater understanding (unless, of course, the student can merely copy the explanation verbatim from the textbook). As another example, in the important area of vocabulary, many instructional and assessment techniques are now available as alternatives to the traditional practice of having students recall or recognize simple definitions. For example, contextual approaches, hierarchical arrays, and linear arrays are all proven alternatives that promote a deeper understanding of word meaning (see, e.g., Beck, Perfetti, & McKeown, 1982; Nagy, 1988).

3. Provide more opportunities for students to write extended answers that require them to synthesize and integrate information across extended text. This recommendation is related to the previous one, because higher order questions

usually require constructed answers that synthesize and integrate information.

4. Ensure that questions are worded clearly and that the recommended answer is reasonable and complete.

We believe that even these few straightforward recommendations would do much to improve the questioning practices in elementary science and social studies materials.

REFERENCES

Andre, T. (1987). Questions and learning from reading. *Questioning Exchange, 1,* 47–86.

Armbruster, B. B., Anderson, T. H., Bruning, R. H., & Meyer, L. A. (1984). *What did you mean by that question?: A taxonomy of American history questions* (Tech. Rep. No. 308). Urbana: University of Illinois, Center for the Study of Reading.

Beck, I. L., Perfetti, C. A., & McKeown, M. G. (1982). Effects of long-term vocabulary instruction on lexical access and reading comprehension. *Journal of Educational Psychology, 74,* 506–521.

Bloom, B. S., Engelhart, M. D., Furst, E. J., Hill, W. H., & Krathwohl, W. H. (1956). *Taxonomy of educational objectives: The classification of educational goals. Handbook I: Cognitive domain.* New York: Longman.

Carrier, C. A., & Fautsch-Patridge, T. (1981). Levels of questions: A framework for the exploration of processing activities. *Contemporary Educational Psychology, 6,* 365–382.

Davis, O. L., Jr., & Hunkins, F. P. (1965). Textbook questions: What thinking processes do they foster? *Peabody Journal of Education, 43,* 285–292.

Dillon, J. T. (1982). The effect of questions in education and other enterprises. *Journal of Curriculum Studies, 14,* 127–152.

Gall, M. D. (1970). The use of questions in teaching. *Review of Educational Research, 40,* 707–721.

Gall, M. D. (1984). Synthesis of research on teacher's questioning. *Educational Leadership, 42,* 40–47.

Hamaker, C. (1986). The effects of adjunct questions on prose learning. *Review of Educational Research, 56,* 212–242.

Nagy, W. E. (1988). *Teaching vocabulary to improve reading comprehension.* Urbana, IL: NCTE and Newark, DE: IRA.

Pearson, P. D., & Johnson, D. D. (1978). *Teaching reading comprehension.* New York: Holt, Rinehart & Winston.

Redfield, D. L., & Rousseau, E. W. (1981). A meta-analysis of experimental research on teacher questioning behavior. *Review of Educational Research, 51,* 237–245.

Rickards, J. (1979). Adjunct postquestions in text: A critical review of methods and processes. *Review of Educational Research, 49,* 181–196.

Rosenshine, B. (1976). Classroom instruction. In N. L. Gage (Ed.), *Psy-*

chology of teaching methods: The seventy-fifth yearbook of the National Society for the Study of Education, Part 1. Chicago: University of Chicago Press.

Smith, R. J., & Barrett, T. C. (1979). Teaching reading in the middle grades (2nd ed.). Reading, MA: Addison-Wesley.

Squire, J. R. (1983). Composing and comprehending: Two sides of the same basic process. Language Arts, 60, 584.

Trachtenberg, D. (1974). Student tasks in text material: What cognitive skills do they tap? Peabody Journal of Education, 52, 54–57.

Tyson-Bernstein, H. (1988). A conspiracy of good intentions: America's textbook fiasco. Washington, DC: The Council for Basic Education.

Valencia, S. V., & Pearson, P. D. (1986). New models for reading assessment (Reading Education Rep. No. 71). Urbana: University of Illinois, Center for the Study of Reading.

Winne, P. H. (1979). Experiments relating teacher's use of higher cognitive questions to student achievement. Review of Educational Research, 49, 13–50.

Wixson, K. K. (1983). Questions about a text: What you ask about is what children learn. The Reading Teacher, 36, 287–293.

Understanding Illustrations in Text

Joel R. Levin
University of Wisconsin, Madison

Richard E. Mayer
University of California, Santa Barbara

Textbook developers have two media available for communicating information: words and pictures or illustrations (Eisenberg, 1978). In spite of our society's bias in favor of verbal over pictorial forms of instruction (Gardner, 1983), a growing research base suggests that text illustrations can have powerful positive effects on students' learning (e.g., Levin, Anglin, & Carney, 1987; Mayer, 1989a). It follows that an effective way to improve the effectiveness of textbooks is to improve the effectiveness of textbook illustrations.

In this chapter, we discuss the substance of which effective text illustrations are made. By effective illustrations, we mean ones that foster positive cognitive outcomes, as reflected by comprehension, memory, and transfer performance. Although it is possible to evaluate illustrations in terms of various noncognitive consequences—for example, aesthetic, attitudinal, or social (e.g., Levie, 1987)—we restrict our attention here to the cognitive consequences of illustrations.

Each of the three major sections of this chapter examines a question suggested by different senses of the term, *understanding illustrations in text*. First, in the sense of whether or not illustrations improve students' understanding of, and learning from, text, we ask a research question: "Do text illustrations improve students' learning?" Second, in the sense of researchers' current understanding of the mechanisms underlying effective illustrations, we ask two related theoretical questions: "Why and when do text illustrations improve students' learning?" Third, in the sense of how to develop textbook illustrations that are more user friendly, considerate, or "understanding" than at present, we ask a practical question: "How can the effectiveness of textbook illustrations be improved?" Several of the specific topics presented in this chapter are extensions and elaborations of the authors' previous discussions, to which the reader is referred (e.g., Levin, 1981, 1989; Mayer, 1989a).

DO TEXT ILLUSTRATIONS IMPROVE STUDENTS' LEARNING?

If there is anything that can be confidently concluded from cognitive psychological research conducted over the last 30 years, it is that pictures are memorable. In countless laboratory learning contexts, a clear finding has emerged: Pictures are remembered far better, and far longer, than are their verbal counterparts (for relevant references and reviews, see Levie, 1987; McDaniel & Pressley, 1987; & Paivio, 1971). This conclusion derives from experimental research paradigms that have incorporated simple, controlled, and often contrived, learning materials (typically, lists of unrelated objects/nouns or object/noun pairs). However, more educationally relevant research conducted within the last 15 years has established a parallel finding: When pictures are incorporated into text material, memory for that material can be substantially improved (see, e.g., Mandl & Levin, 1989; & Willows & Houghton, 1987). It is this latter collection of research findings to which we now turn.

There was a time when it was widely accepted by reading educators and reading researchers that pictures were detrimental to the reading process. That was because the distinction had not yet been clearly made between learning to read (the initial reading skills of decoding and word identification) and reading to learn (the later reading skills of comprehending and remembering text content). An influential review by Samuels (1970) provided substantial ammunition for those who believed that text-accompanying illustrations are more harmful than helpful. As has been pointed out previously, however (Levin, 1983; Levin et al., 1987), Samuels' review focused primarily on the learning-to-read stage—a stage that research has indeed found to be adversely affected by the addition of pictures.

In contrast, in more recent years, the inclusion of illustrations with a reading-to-learn intent has been found repeatedly to be beneficial, leading to the unequivocal assertion that the addition of illustrations to a text can improve students' learning from that text, sometimes substantially (e.g., Levie & Lentz, 1982; Levin et al., 1987; Schallert, 1980). For example, in a recent meta-analytic review of the illustrations-in-text literature, Levin et al. (1987) found that across all empirical studies that compared text plus illustrations with text alone (resulting in 75 comparisons), the average illustration facilitation amounted to better than .8 standard deviations—an "effect size" that Cohen (1977) and others regard as "large."

Note we stated that illustrations can improve learning from text. This suggests that illustrations are not globally effective under all conditions. Exactly why and when illustrations positively affect the reading-to-learn process are what we intend to speculate about here, for those two questions comprise the crux of this chapter.

WHY DO TEXT ILLUSTRATIONS IMPROVE STUDENTS' LEARNING?

There are likely many competing, as well as complementary, explanations for why text comprehension and recall are facilitated by pictorial supplements. Stemming from our previous considerations (Levin, 1981; Mayer, 1989a), we have catalogued seven such explanations, each beginning with the letter "C." And so, we seize this opportunity to sell the seven Cs.

Seven Proposed Explanations of Illustration Efficacy

Text-accompanying illustrations have been posited to improve learning as a result of their making text information more:

• *concentrated* or focused, by bringing the most critical text information to the learner's attention. This characteristic reflects what both Mayer (1989a) and Larkin and Simon (1987) regarded as a *selection* function of pictures. That is, carefully crafted illustrations can communicate the essence of what is to be understood and remembered of text, thereby relieving the learner of the responsibility of discriminating between more- and less-important text information.

• *compact/concise*, by converting a "thousand words" into a more informationally efficient form. The following verbal description, taken from Larkin and Simon (1987), certainly provides a very complete, though not very compact, representation of a pulley system. (Please refrain from looking at the corresponding diagram until you have read the verbal description.)

> We have three pulleys, two weights, and some ropes, arranged as follows: 1. The first weight is suspended from the left end of a rope over Pulley *A*. The right end of this rope is attached to, and partially supports, the second weight. 2. Pulley *A* is suspended from the left end of a rope that runs over Pulley *B*, and under Pulley *C*. Pulley *B* is suspended from the ceiling. The right end of the rope that runs under Pulley *C* is attached to the ceiling. 3. Pulley *C* is attached to the second weight, supporting it jointly with the right end of the first rope. (Larkin & Simon, 1987, p. 72)

Can you picture that pulley system in your mind's eye? Now get the real picture in Fig. 4.1. (You may look now!) In this case, you would probably agree that the picture is more than worth the 100 words.

• *concrete*, by providing a more picturable representation of the text content. Enhancing text concreteness is associated with Levin's (1981) *representation* function of illustrations. The characters and events of concrete narrative passages become even more concrete through the addition of visual illustrations; and so do the descriptions and expositions of nonnarrative texts. Closely aligned with this explanation are Paivio's (e.g., 1986) arguments that concrete stimuli (such as pictures) produce *combined* ("dually coded") pictorial–verbal internal representations of those stimuli, which are posited to be more meaningful and memorable than are singly coded verbal representations.

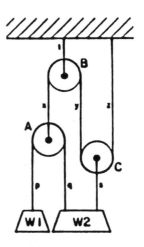

FIG. 4.1 Representational illustration of a pulley system (from Larkin & Simon, 1987).

* *coherent,* by organizing or structuring the text in a more systematic fashion. Coherence corresponds to Levin's (1981) *organization* function, and is also clearly compatible with our previously mentioned *compactness/conciseness* construct. Pictorial organization makes a text more "internally connected" (Mayer, 1989a). With poorly structured texts—or for students who fail to capitalize on a text's structure—illustrations can provide a coherent organization. In the domains of social studies and science, for example, coherence is often effected through the provision of maps, graphs, flowcharts, and figural taxonomies (e.g., Abel & Kulhavy, 1986; Eylon & Reif, 1984; Winn, 1987).

* *comprehensible,* by turning a complex, difficult-to-interpret text into one that is easier to understand. This is Levin's (1981) *interpretation* function, and it applies primarily to texts that are relatively unintelligible to the uninitiated learner. Science and other technical material often fit that bill, even when such material is presumably packaged for general consumption. For example, consider the following *Newsweek* excerpt relating to the 1989 cold-fusion phenomenon. (Again, please do not look at the accompanying illustration until you have read the excerpt.)

Palladium encircled by platinum is placed in "heavy" water, in which hydrogen is replaced by deuterium. Electricity separates oxygen from deuterium, which is absorbed by palladium. The deuterium atoms are squeezed into the palladium's latticelike structure. Eventually they fuse, releasing energy and, in some experiments, neutrons and a form of helium. (Begley, 1989, p. 50)

Assuming that you, the reader, are a "normal" human being (i.e., a nonchemist or a nonphysicist), we certainly excuse your cold-fusion confusion. Such confusion may be somewhat defused, however, by taking a look at Fig. 4.2. (You may open your eyes now.)

Illustrations that serve to simplify complex scientific concepts often take the form of pictorial models (as in Fig. 4.2). Examples of pictorial models that have proven to be effective empirically are those developed by Mayer (1989b) for brakes (see Fig. 4.3), by Dwyer (1968) for the circulatory system, and by Hurt (1987) for photosynthesis.

• *correspondent,* by constructing pictorial relationships between unfamiliar concepts and those with which the learner is already familiar. Correspondence captures Mayer's (1989a) *integration* function as it directly applies to "building external connections," and an effective way of building such connections often involves the creative application of pictorial analogies. Empirically documented examples include Hurt's (1987) "bell-ringer" analogy for human muscles (see Fig. 4.4), Mayer's (1980) "office filing-system" analogy for data-based management, and Bromage and Mayer's (1981) "eye" analogy for the aperture of a camera. Correspondence can be closely coordinated with comprehensibility, in that the provision of pictorial analogies (correspon-

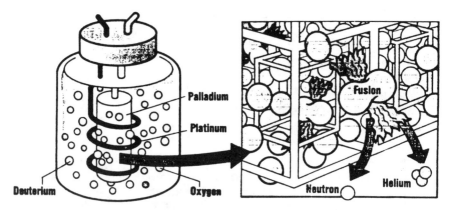

FIG. 4.2   Model illustration for *cold fusion* (from Begley, 1989).

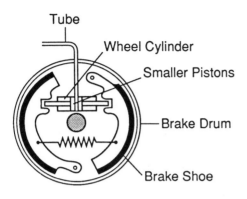

Tube
Wheel Cylinder
Smaller Pistons
Brake Drum
Brake Shoe

When the driver steps on the car's brake pedal...

A piston moves forward inside the master cylinder (not shown).

The piston forces brake fluid out of the master cylinder and through the tubes to the wheel cylinders.

In the wheel cylinders, the increase in fluid pressure makes a set of smaller pistons move.

When the brake shoes press against the drum both the drum and the wheel stop or slow down.

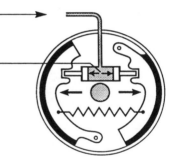

FIG. 4.3 Model illustration for *hydraulic drum brakes* (from Mayer, 1989b. Adapted from *The World Book Encyclopedia.* © 1992 World Book, Inc. By permission of publisher).

dence) represents a figurative means of rendering an abstruse text more comprehensible.

• *codable,* by capitalizing on pictorial mnemonic (memory enhancing) techniques to make difficult-to-remember text content more memorable (see, e.g., Levin, 1982). Mnemonic pictures (Levin's, 1981, *transformation* function) transform unfamiliar text-embedded names, terminology, or facts into a more memorable pictorial form. For example, in a passage describing a plant classification system, the unfamiliar term *angiosperm* (a flower-bearing plant) could be recoded as the orthographically similar word *angel,* and then illustrated as an angel holding a bunch of flowers, as in Fig. 4.5 (e.g., Rosenheck, Levin, & Levin, 1989). Empirically, mnemonic

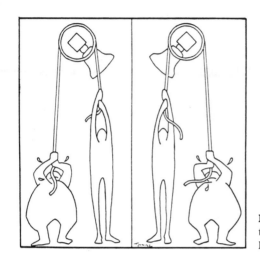

FIG. 4.4 Analogical illustration for *human muscles* (from Hurt, 1987).

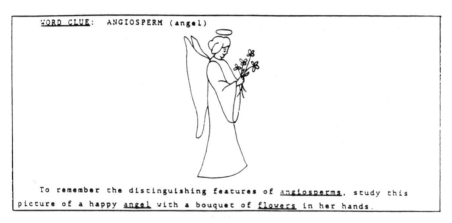

WORD CLUE: ANGIOSPERM (angel)

To remember the distinguishing features of angiosperms, study this picture of a happy angel with a bouquet of flowers in her hands.

FIG. 4.5 Mnemonic illustration for *angiosperm* (from Rosenheck et al., 1989. Copyright © 1989 by the APA. Reprinted by permission).

illustrations have been found to dramatically improve students' acquisition of social studies and science content, including facts about people and places (e.g., Peters & Levin, 1986), mineral attributes (Levin, Morrison, McGivern, Mastropieri, & Scruggs, 1986), and even the reasons for dinosaur extinction (Mastropieri, Scruggs, & Levin, 1987). And recently, along with mnemonic illustrations to improve students' memory for unfamiliar plant terminology (such as *angiosperm, conopsida,* and *taxales*), a mnemonic pictorial taxonomy (a *mnemonomy*) was developed to facilitate college students' ability, both to remember and to apply a variety of plant classification information (Levin & Levin, 1990; Rosenheck et al., 1989).

These, then, represent seven possible "whys" of illustration potency. Finally, we include an eighth memorial benefit of illustrations, namely the one that enhances a people's:

• *collective* recollection, as is the case with such vivid, deeply implanted icons as: the atom bomb's mushroom-shaped cloud; John Kennedy, Jr., as a young boy, saluting during his father's funeral procession; a graphic Vietnam execution; or Neil Armstrong's first steps on the moon (see, e.g., *Time* magazine's, fall, 1989, special issue on 150 years of photojournalism). Such never-to-be-forgotten snapshots in the brain are part of our nation's—and indeed, the world's— pictorial-memorial legacy.

Summary

Why do illustrations improve learning from text? The preceding *C*s encapsulate several separate and overlapping proposed "explanations." Which explanations are correct or best, nobody knows. There is likely some truth to all of them, or varying degrees of truth, depending on the specific conditions surrounding the use of illustrations (as is discussed). In particular, the word "explanations" has been put in quotes here, inasmuch as precious little research on the precise characteristics and cognitive mechanisms associated with text-enhancing illustrations has been conducted (Mandl & Levin, 1989). But our armchair analysis could provide an impetus for formulating some testable hypotheses; and now that we have considered some of the "whys" of illustration efficacy, let us move on to the "whens."

WHEN DO TEXT ILLUSTRATIONS IMPROVE STUDENTS' LEARNING?

In this section, we focus on the conditions under which text illustrations are likely to be helpful. In parallel with Bransford's (1979) *tetrahedral* model, these conditions encompass: (a) the desired performance outcomes, as well as characteristics of (b) the illustrations, (c) the text, and (d) the learner. We view performance outcomes as the natural point from which all other characteristics depart, and so, naturally, that is the point from which we will depart.

Performance Outcomes

The first condition for effective illustrations is that the illustrations must be appropriate for the type of performance test that the learner will be taking. A fundamental assumption, which has been presented and supported in our previous work, is that a given instructional aid or strategy cannot be expected to be uniformly effective with respect to all possible performance outcomes (see, e.g., Levin, 1989; & Mayer, 1989a). In this context, the general question: "Are text illustrations effective?" must be replaced with the more task-specific question: "For which cognitive outcomes are text illustrations effective?" Chief among the cognitive outcomes that can be considered are those that reflect a learner's: (a) understanding or comprehension of a passage during text processing, (b) remembering specific passage information during text retrieval, and (c) applying what has been learned in the service of creative thinking on "transfer" tasks requiring inference and problem solving (Levin, 1986).

We provide a few salient illustrations of these differential performance-outcome notions. Certain types of text illustrations clearly promote understanding, especially when the to-be-processed text content is dense, difficult, or disconnected. Think back to the palladium example provided earlier, and how the accompanying illustration may have helped you enhance your comprehension of the cold-fusion description. Yet, even with that enhanced understanding—and without looking back at the passage—can you remember: "What surrounds palladium in the "heavy water?" "What replaces hydrogen?" "What does electricity separate from deuterium?" "What is released following fusion?" Perhaps you can answer these questions, but probably you can not. Why not? It is because the information contained in the passage was likely quite unfamiliar to you (and, therefore, difficult to remember), and the illustration does not provide the explicit connections needed to facilitate your retrieval of that information. Thus, this subjective example is one in which an illustration may have improved your understanding, though not your recall, of the palladium-passage content.

As a few empirical research examples of the differential performance enhancement of text illustrations: (a) Abel and Kulhavy (1986) found that pictorial maps improved students' recall of picture-relevant information, but not of picture-irrelevant information (consistent with our "text relatedness" principle, discussed in the next section); (b) Hurt (1987) found that simple pictorial models were more beneficial for text information that could be directly pictured than for text information that could not be directly pictured, whereas the reverse was true for pictorial analogies; (c) Levin's research has demonstrated that mnemonic illustrations improve students' associative (linked) memory for text information, though not their nonassociative memory (e.g., Levin, Shriberg, & Berry, 1983; Mastropieri, Scruggs, & Levin, 1987); and (d) Mayer has repeatedly found that under certain conditions, pictorial models and analogies improve students' conceptual understanding and problem solving, but not their verbatim memory for text information (e.g., Bromage & Mayer, 1981; Mayer, 1989b).

Illustration Characteristics

The second condition for effective illustrations is that the illustrations must be related to the text, and that the illustrations must be of sufficient character and quality that they are perceived by the learner as being related to the text.

Text Relatedness. It has now been well established that in order for text-accompanying illustrations to be effective, the illustrations must be related to the text content. This text-relatedness principle can be satisfied by different types of pictures. For example, both directly related representational, organizational, and model illustrations, as well as less directly related analogical and mnemonic illustrations, can improve students' learning from text. Clearly, however, illustrations that function as no more than attractive "decorational" devices (Levin, 1981), bearing no relationship whatsoever to the text content, do not satisfy the principle. Bolstering these claims are the empirical findings that, whereas all types of text-related illustration do indeed improve various aspects of students' learning from text, text-unrelated illustrations do not (Levin et al., 1987).

Perceived Text Relatedness. Even more critical than text relatedness as defined by the text provider (i.e., the illustrator, educator, or researcher), is text relatedness as perceived by the text processor (i.e., the student). Thus, if a nominally text-related illustration is not processed in the intended way, then: (a) the illustration must be regarded as functionally text-unrelated, and (b) learning gains will not likely result. A few recent investigations serve to support these assumptions (e.g., Guri, 1985; Issing, Hannemann, & Haack, 1989; Weidenmann, 1989). Weidenmann, for example, found that college students who were instructed to attend to specific cues in text-accompanying pictures subsequently recalled more text information than did students who were presented pictures without cuing instructions. Moreover, whereas the picture-instructed students outrecalled no-picture control subjects, picture-uninstructed students did not outrecall no-picture controls.

Illustration Quality. The artistic quality of an illustration likely affects both a student's initial interpretation of the illustration and the illustration's subsequent effect on learning. Although a good deal of research has investigated the issue of picture form (e.g., realistic illustrations, schematic illustrations, black-and-white photographs, color photographs), almost none has investigated the issue of picture quality per se (see, e.g., Levie, 1987).

Text Characteristics

The third condition for effective illustrations is that the text itself be related to the illustrations and that the text characteristics are compatible with the kind of illustrations provided.

Illustration Relatedness. By focusing on the text rather than the illustration, we can apply a second relatedness principle. Specifically, a learner must be capable of extracting a certain amount of basic text information in order to perceive the text as picture-related (unless, of course, a provided illustration is so self-contained that it will function well independently of nominal text processing). Clearly, for example, at least some degree of word decoding and word recognition, and semantic integration proficiency, is necessary for any text processing to be taking place (as is discussed under "Learner Characteristics"). This point appears to be especially apropos in cases where young children and less-skilled readers are the text processors who may "fail to see the pictures for the prose."

Text Type, Complexity, Coherence, and Information Density. Assuming that the aforementioned text-processing skills are present, however, a reasonable assumption is that the more complex the concepts are in the text, the more likely it is that illustrations (i.e., pictorial models and analogies) will be helpful. Similarly, the more poorly structured the text, the more beneficial the organizational maps, flowcharts, or taxonomies should be; the more unfamiliar factual information there is to remember in the text, the more facilitative mnemonic illustrations should be.

The general message here is that different types of texts, and even different aspects of a particular text, will likely benefit maximally from different types of illustrations. With respect to narrative texts there are questions of whether to illustrate and how to illustrate higher level themes versus lower level details. For explanatory scientific texts, the same questions arise with respect to structure versus function, parts versus wholes, labels versus attributes, relationships versus details, and so on. For example, in most of Mayer's research on pictorial models, a complete system or process (e.g., radar, Ohm's Law, the nitrogen cycle, brakes) was illustrated (Mayer, 1989a). In contrast, in Levin's research with pictorial mnemonics, individual part or component information (e.g., hardness levels, colors, and uses of specific minerals; interrelationships and defining characteristics of specific plants) was illustrated (Levin, 1988). To date, speculations about which illustration types are most effective for which types of text and text information remain largely untested, however (also see Haring & Fry, 1979; Hurt, 1987; Levin, Shriberg, & Berry, 1983; & Waddill, McDaniel, & Einstein, 1988).

Learner Characteristics

The final condition for effective illustrations is that the learner possess the appropriate knowledge and skills to profit from the illustrations.

Learner Knowledge. For any text or segment of text, different learners may be assumed to possess different pre-existing levels of topic-relevant (domain-specific) knowledge. For certain text types, such differences may be expected to be predictive of the degree to which illustrations will be helpful. For example, Mayer (1989a) documented that students with high background knowledge in a particular scientific domain do not benefit from pictorial models as much as do students with low background knowledge.

On the other hand (and consistent with our *perceived text relatedness* principle), a learner must possess the knowledge needed to extract from an illustration that which was intended by the illustrator. Consider, for example, a learner who has no background knowledge of the vehicle being used to provide a pictorial analogy. Thus, if a learner has no concept of a weaver's loom, to what extent will she or he be able to capitalize on a loom analogy in order to understand and remember Melville's "Mat Maker" passage from *Moby Dick* (Davidson, 1976)?

Learner Skills. Included here are the learner's text-processing and text-retrieval skills, as well as the learner's picture-processing and picture-retrieval skills. Consideration of these text and picture skills leads to several plausible predictions. As a few specific examples, it would be expected that: (a) students must have adequate basic reading skills in order to relate the text information to a provided illustration (the perceived *illustration-relatedness* principle); (b) students must be able to understand an illustration in order to relate it to the text (the perceived *text-relatedness* principle); and (c) students with poor text-comprehension skills are likely to benefit more from comprehension-enhancing illustrations than are more skilled comprehenders.

Summary

In summary, text-accompanying illustrations will likely be effective when: (a) they can be mapped directly onto specific learning outcomes, (b) they are related to the text, and (c) they are well suited to the unique characteristics of the learner. Moreover: (d) different types of texts and illustrations can be expected to produce different degrees of text-learning facilitation. These conditions should not be considered separately from one another. Rather, interactions among the aforementioned four conditions can and should be anticipated. Especially relevant interactions are those involving the type of illustration provided (e.g., model, analogical, mnemonic) as related to the specified learning outcomes, as well as to both text and learner characteristics.

HOW CAN THE EFFECTIVENESS OF TEXTBOOK ILLUSTRATIONS BE IMPROVED?

In this section, we turn to the practical issue of how to design text illustrations that are effective with respect to the cognitive outcomes of understanding, remembering, and applying text information. Our recommendations follow directly from the theoretical and empirical research literature on the "whys" and "whens" of text illustration, as already reflected, respectively, in our seven explanatory *C* criteria and four text-learning conditions (performance outcomes, and illustration, text, and learner characteristics).

Recommendation 1. Clearly define the kind of criterion performance that is desired of the student. Do you want the student to understand dense or conceptually difficult material, to remember unfamiliar content, or to transfer text concepts in novel or creative ways? Given an *understanding* goal, concise pictorial representations (Fig. 4.1) or comprehensible pictorial models (Figs. 4.2 and 4.3) and analogies (Fig. 4.4) may be useful. Given a *remembering* goal, connected pictorial organizations (such as maps, flowcharts, and taxonomies) and, especially, recoded mnemonic illustrations (Fig. 4.5) are likely appropriate. And given an *applying* goal, illustrations that foster factual and conceptual transfer are indicated, as has been empirically documented with appropriately constructed model, analogical, and mnemonic illustrations (Levin, 1988; Mayer, 1989a).

Recommendation 2. Determine whether the illustrations include the specific functional characteristics desired and are of the desired quality. Text-unrelated illustrations may help to sell textbooks or to beautify them, but such illustrations will not improve students' processing or retrieval of the text information. Illustrations that are not interpreted by students in the manner intended by the illustrator will be similarly ineffectual from a cognitive outcome standpoint.

Recommendation 3.   Analyze the text with respect to its organizational structure and complexity in order to assess whether illustrations are needed and what kinds of illustrations are needed. Easy-to-follow, concrete, narrative passages or descriptive essays most likely require no illustrations at all; whereas complex, unfamiliar, explanatory science texts may well benefit from the inclusion of comprehension- or memory-enhancing illustrations (of the model, analogical, or mnemonic variety). Wordy descriptions of scientific systems or processes can often be made easier to understand through the provision of more compact pictorial representations.

Recommendation 4.   Be aware of the knowledge and skills of the learners for whom the text is intended, and develop illustrations in accordance with that awareness. As a rule of thumb: (a) the less background knowledge possessed by the student in the particular topic domain covered, and (b) the less proficient the student is at verbal information processing (generally, younger students and those with learning difficulties), the greater the potential benefit of a text-relevant illustration. At the same time, a student must possess the requisite knowledge and skills: (a) to capitalize on the desired literal and figural interpretations of an illustration, and (b) to perceive picture/text connections through the deployment of adequate word recognition and picture perception processes. If a student is weak in any of these capabilities, an illustration will fall short of its potential effectiveness.

Concluding Comments

There is clearly a need for the development of more, and more effective, textbook illustrations. For illustrations to be more effective, however, they must be selected wisely, in relation to both the desired performance outcomes and specific text and learner characteristics. With continued research and logical analyses of the kind presented in this chapter, we are optimistic that students, educational researchers, and instructional designers will all be on much firmer ground with respect to understanding text illustrations.

ACKNOWLEDGMENT

We are grateful to Mary E. Levin for her comments on an earlier version of this manuscript.

REFERENCES

Abel, R. R., & Kulhavy, R. W. (1986). Maps, mode of text presentation, and children's prose learning. *American Educational Research Journal, 23,* 263–274.

Begley, S. (1989, May 8). The race for fusion. *Newsweek,* pp. 48–54.

Bransford, J. D. (1979). *Human cognition: Learning, understanding, and remembering.* Belmont, CA: Wadsworth.

Bromage, B. K., & Mayer, R. E. (1981). Relationship between what is remembered and creative problem solving performance in science learning. *Journal of Educational Psychology, 73,* 451–461.

Cohen, J. (1977). *Statistical power analysis for the behavioral sciences* (2nd ed.). New York: Academic Press.

Davidson, R. E. (1976). The role of metaphor and analogy in learning. In J. R. Levin & V. L. Allen (Eds.), *Cognitive learning in children: Theories and strategies* (pp. 135–162). New York: Academic Press.

Dwyer, F. M., Jr. (1968). The effectiveness of selected visual illustrations in teaching science concepts to college freshmen. *Journal of Educational Research, 61,* 343–347.

Eisenberg, A. (1978). *Reading technical books.* Englewood Cliffs, NJ: Prentice-Hall.

Eylon, B.-S., & Reif, F. (1984). Effects of knowledge organization on task performance. *Cognition and Instruction, 1,* 5–44.

Gardner, H. (1983). *Frames of mind.* New York: Basic.

Guri, S. (1985, March-April). *The function of diagrams in learning from social science self-study texts.* Paper presented at the annual meeting of the American Educational Research Association, Chicago.

Haring, M. J., & Fry, M. A. (1979). Effect of pictures on children's comprehension of written text. *Educational Communication and Technology Journal, 27,* 185–190.

Hurt, J. A. (1987). Assessing functional effectiveness of pictorial representations used in text. *Educational Communication and Technology Journal, 35,* 85–94.

Issing, L. J., Hannemann, J., & Haack, J. (1989). Visualization by pictorial analogies in understanding expository text. In H. Mandl & J. R. Levin (Eds.), *Knowledge acquisition from text and pictures* (pp. 195–214). Amsterdam: Elsevier.

Larkin, J. H., & Simon, H. A. (1987). Why a diagram is (sometimes) worth ten thousand words. *Cognitive Science, 11*, 65–99.

Levie, W. H. (1987). Research on pictures: A guide to the literature. In D. M. Willows & H. A. Houghton (Eds.), *The psychology of illustration: I. Basic research* (pp. 1–50). New York: Springer-Verlag.

Levie, W. H., & Lentz, R. (1982). Effects of text illustrations: A review of research. *Educational Communication and Technology Journal, 30,* 195–232.

Levin, J. R. (1981). On functions of pictures in prose. In F. J. Pirozzolo & M. C. Wittrock (Eds.), *Neuropsychological and cognitive processes in reading* (pp. 203–228). New York: Academic Press.

Levin, J. R. (1982). Pictures as prose-learning devices. In A. Flammer & W. Kintsch (Eds.), *Discourse processing* (pp. 412–444). Amsterdam: North-Holland.

Levin, J. R. (1983). Pictorial strategies for school learning: Practical illustrations. In M. Pressley & J. R. Levin (Eds.), *Cognitive strategy research: Educational applications* (pp. 213–237). New York: Springer-Verlag.

Levin, J. R. (1986). Four cognitive principles of learning-strategy instruction. *Educational Psychologist, 21,* 3–17.

Levin, J. R. (1988, April). *Thinking about and with memory strategies.* Paper presented at the annual meeting of the American Educational Research Association, New Orleans.

Levin, J. R. (1989). A transfer-appropriate-processing perspective of pictures in prose. In H. Mandl & J. R. Levin (Eds.), *Knowledge acquisition from text and pictures* (pp. 83–100). Amsterdam: Elsevier.

Levin, J. R., Anglin, G. J., & Carney, R. N. (1987). On empirically validating functions of pictures in prose. In D. M. Willows & H. A. Houghton (Eds.), *The psychology of illustration: I. Basic research* (pp. 51–85). New York: Springer-Verlag.

Levin, M. E., & Levin, J. R. (1990). Scientific mnemonomies: Methods for maximizing more than memory. *American Educational Research Journal, 27,* 301–321.

Levin, J. R., Morrison, C. R., McGivern, J. E., Mastropieri, M. A., & Scruggs, T. E. (1986). Mnemonic facilitation of text-embedded science facts. *American Educational Research Journal, 23,* 489–506.

Levin, J. R., Shriberg, L. K., & Berry, J. K. (1983). A concrete strategy for remembering abstract prose. *American Educational Research Journal, 20,* 277–290.

Mandl, H., & Levin, J. R. (Eds.). (1989). *Knowledge acquisition from text and pictures.* Amsterdam: Elsevier.

Mastropieri, M. A., Scruggs, T. E., & Levin, J. R. (1987). Learning-disabled students' memory for expository prose: Mnemonic versus nonmnemonic pictures. *American Educational Research Journal, 24,* 505–519.

Mayer, R. E. (1980). Elaboration techniques that increase the meaningfulness of technical text: An experimental test of the learning strategy hypothesis. *Journal of Educational Psychology, 72,* 770–784.

Mayer, R. E. (1989a). Models for understanding. *Review of Educational Research, 59,* 43–64.

Mayer, R. E. (1989b). Systematic thinking fostered by illustrations in scientific text. *Journal of Educational Psychology, 81,* 240–246.

McDaniel, M. A., & Pressley, M. (Eds.). (1987). *Imagery and related mnemonic processes: Theories, individual differences, and applications.* New York: Springer-Verlag.

Paivio, A. (1971). *Imagery and verbal processes.* Hillsdale, NJ: Lawrence Erlbaum Associates.

Paivio, A. (1986). *Mental representations: A dual-coding approach.* New York: Oxford University Press.

Peters, E. E., & Levin, J. R. (1986). Effects of a mnemonic imagery strategy on good and poor readers' prose recall. *Reading Research Quarterly, 21,* 179–192.

Rosenheck, M. B., & Levin, M. E., & Levin, J. R. (1989). Learning botany concepts mnemonically: Seeing the forest and the trees. *Journal of Educational Psychology, 81,* 196–203.

Samuels, S. J. (1970). Effects of pictures on learning to read, comprehension and attitudes. *Review of Educational Research, 40,* 397–407.

Schallert, D. L. (1980). The role of illustrations in reading comprehension. In R. J. Spiro, B. C. Bruce, & W. F. Brewer (Eds.), *Theoretical issues in reading comprehension: Perspectives from cognitive psychology, linguistics, artificial intelligence, and education.* Hillsdale, NJ: Lawrence Erlbaum Associates.

Waddill, P. J., McDaniel, M. A., & Einstein, G. O. (1988). Illustrations as adjuncts to prose: A text-appropriate processing approach. *Journal of Educational Psychology, 80,* 457–464.

Weidenmann, B. (1989). When good pictures fail: An information-processing approach to the effect of illustrations. In H. Mandl & J. R. Levin (Eds.), *Knowledge acquisition from text and pictures* (pp. 157–171). Amsterdam: Elsevier.

Willows, D. M., & Houghton, H. A. (Eds.). (1987). *The psychology of illustration: I. Basic research.* New York: Springer-Verlag.

Winn, B. (1987). Charts, graphs and diagrams in educational materials. In D. M. Willows & H. A. Houghton (Eds.), *The psychology of illustration: I. Basic research* (pp. 152–198). New York: Springer-Verlag.

■ 5 ■

Do Illustrations Serve an Instructional Purpose in U.S. Textbooks?

Arthur Woodward
Research, Development and Outreach Center
of The Norman Howard School, NY

By definition, textbooks attempt to distill and interpret the knowledge and scholarship of a discipline. They attempt to provide an overview of a field in sufficient breadth and depth that students can begin to understand what the discipline is about, and the methodologies and scholarship that underpin it. Thus, textbooks represent what is known about a discipline, modified according to the needs, knowledge, and maturity of the anticipated audience. Textbooks, then, are a standard resource, reference, and instructional tool, and so it is not surprising that it is from these instructional materials that teachers teach and students learn. Across grade levels in U.S. schools, in subjects as diverse as American history, chemistry, and health, and at various grade levels, the likelihood is that textbooks are the primary instructional material.

Books, and by extension textbooks, command a special respect. Teachers use textbooks to structure their teaching; students expect to have textbooks for each class; and parents are upset if their children do not use this instructional material that earlier helped define their own educational experiences. At first glance, textbooks are quite impressive. They have the "heft" one associates with learned books, combined with a color and design quality that make them visually appealing. In addition, modern textbooks offer a cornacopia of features; they seem to cover all the topics that make up a particular subject; they are copiously and color- fully illustrated; and they contain many extras, such as glossaries, workbooks, and supplements.

On closer inspection however, scholars have found that textbooks published in the United States are often unde- serving of the respect accorded them (Ravitch, 1987; Sewall, 1988; Tyson & Woodward, 1989b). These researchers found that many textbooks are written in overly simplistic and choppy prose, contain design features that serve marketing rather than instructional purposes, and cover too many topics and concepts too superficially.

One aspect of the current critique of the instructional quality of textbooks involves illustrations. In this chapter the following topics are discussed: (a) how social and political forces have influenced the type and number of illustrations in textbooks, (b) the marketing forces that have influenced the textbooks publishers produce, (c) the instructional effective- ness of illustrations in contemporary textbooks, and (d) the influence—or rather, the lack of influence—of research on practice.

THE MARKET

Textbooks are the result of a complex marketplace that includes numerous consumers, including those who seek to influence what is consumed, and a small group of publishers who attempt to respond to market demands. These pub- lishers are very successful in satisfying the demands of the market and they are able to develop "consensus" textbooks for each subject area. These consensus textbooks are de- signed to be sold nationwide and seem to satisfy the demands of different parties—those states that have formal and cen- tralized adoption policies, or suburban, rural, or city school districts that adopt textbooks free from state control. Not surprisingly, these consensus textbooks tend to be very similar in design and content, for each publisher attempts to sell to the same market. When publishers do change text- books, the likelihood is that these changes will be in modest, rather than radical increments. If textbook changes are met with market approval, then other publishers will quickly follow suit.

The notion of a national marketplace served by a small group of publishers—and the consensus implied in this relationship—has serious consequences for the design of textbooks and the use of illustrations. At the root of the problem is the fact that textbooks must represent the market consensus. In other words, an elementary school reading series must be acceptable in states as diverse as Georgia and New York; it must be acceptable in rural, suburban, and city districts; the series must pass hurdles created by agencies concerned with issues of social and political representation; and it must meet the requirements imposed by those states and local school districts that adopt textbooks.

Even though consensus textbooks exist, can they really meet the needs of the myriad consumers that make up the market? These districts serve different populations, have different instructional philosophies, and, in many cases, have curricula that are quite different. It follows then that consensus must be based on something other than content and instructional design, for textbooks designed for the national market cannot, by definition, adequately meet the needs of its various constituents.

The consensus about textbooks is based on such factors as (a) breadth of topic coverage (i.e., textbooks will appear to cover every topic on a district's curriculum), (b) ease of use (i.e., teachers' guides will provide for every teaching eventuality), (c) the importance of photographs and other illustrations, (d) the inclusion of testing and activity components, and (e) the representation of women and minorities (primarily through illustrations). Interestingly, these very features have been severely criticized by researchers for contributing to poor quality textbooks. As I (Woodward, 1987) noted, these features have often become "proxies" for textbook quality.

ILLUSTRATIONS AND THE MARKETPLACE

One of the most obvious features about textbooks is not the words they contain but their illustrations. Illustrations in elementary, secondary, and recently, even introductory college textbooks, are bountiful, impressive, and almost over-whelming. Indeed, contemporary textbooks are more colorful and startlingly beautiful than even a few years ago. One can hardly open a textbook and not find a four-color photograph or other illustration that immediately catches the eye. The very number and quality of illustrations gives one pause; are these illustrations really necessary for helping students learn the concepts and content of a particular discipline or do they serve some other noninstructional purpose? This doubt is reinforced by the results of studies by Evans, Watson, and Willows (1987) and O'Brien (1988), who found that teachers expect textbooks to be richly illustrated. At the same time, although teachers reported that they use illustrations in their instruction, observations indicated that teachers rarely used textbook illustrations in teaching. Textbook publishers and editors were also interviewed by Evans et al., and these publishing executives felt compelled to match the quantity and quality of illustrations of competitive publishers.

The specific marketing functions of illustrations include: (a) the use of illustrations to attract attention and create positive affect, (b) the substitution of color for black-and-white illustrations, and (c) the use of illustrations for social policy purposes. These are discussed in turn.

The Use of Illustrations to Attract Attention and Create Positive Affect

From the cover of a textbook to the number of four-color illustrations that can be found on almost every page, the marketing function of illustrations is to encourage selectors to pick up, thumb through, and hopefully review and select a particular book or series. The attractiveness of a book becomes an important factor in the textbook selection process. Generally, selection committees are poorly trained in evaluation techniques and have little time to complete the task, so illustrations, combined with other criteria, can become a convenient and quick way of making a selection decision.

Because copyright date becomes an important selection criteria (many educators balk at choosing a textbook 1 or 2 years old), changing covers and illustrations serve to indicate a "new" textbook. However, Woodward and Nagel (1987, 1988) found very few changes in elementary social studies textbooks from one copyright date to another, except when textbooks underwent major revisions (perhaps once every 5 or 6 years). Not unreasonably, publishers find it difficult to make substantial and frequent content changes in their textbooks. To give the appearance of new books, the publishers change covers and illustrations.

The Substitution of Color for Black-and-White Illustrations

Color illustrations are now considered a standard feature of textbooks and are increasingly used to replace black-and-white photographs. Unfortunately, this substitution may result in illustrations that are instructionally less effective than the ones they replaced. For example, across editions of a fifth-grade, social studies textbook Woodward and Nagel (1987, 1988) found that a black-and-white print depicting the squalid living quarters of slaves as they relaxed during some rare free time had been replaced with a romanticized, Corot-like painting depicting slaves at leisure. In another case, a black-and-white print showing a grim slave auction was replaced with a color print of an auction where women slaves were dressed in nicely starched white aprons and gingham gowns.

In the same textbooks, a chapter on industrial and agricultural development contained a black-and-white photograph of New York's Flatiron Building under construction amidst the bustle of urban life. The black-and-white photograph showed a horse-drawn cart, and working men and women; it gave an impression of what it was like to be in a thriving city during that period. In the later edition, this photograph was replaced with a color photograph—an aerial view of the Flatiron Building, more appropriate for a magazine advertisement or an architect's rendering than as an image reflecting the text's content.

The Use of Illustrations for Social Policy and Political Purposes

In response to legitimate complaints in the 1960s and 1970s that textbooks failed to include photographs of women and minorities, publishing companies attempted to correct the

imbalance of illustrations in their publications. This adjust-
ment was hastened when many states adopted laws man-
dating that textbooks first had to meet criteria regarding
portrayals of women and minority groups in order to be
selected. Unfortunately, methods of meeting this require-
ment have often degenerated into counting illustrations instead of evaluating them for verisimilitude and instructional
effectiveness. Thus, with quantity of illustrations rather than
overall quality of the illustrations and text as a selection
criteria, publishing companies peppered their textbooks with
photographs of women and members of minority groups in
the roles of coalminers, crane operators, judges, politicians,
and so forth—whether or not these illustrations were related
to the text in some meaningful way or reflected reality. In
many cases, the inclusion of these illustrations amounted to
a new form of tokenism.

Illustrations can be an important political element in responding to a particular market. For example, key adoption
states such as Texas and California are well represented in
textbooks. Photographs such as the Texas state capitol in a
chapter on minerals in an elementary science book or a
California Civic Center in a chapter on local government in a
civics text are quite common. These illustrations do not
relate to or reinforce the content and concepts in the text.
Rather, they seem to function to reassure important adoption
states that textbook content is influenced by, if not specifically tailored to, their needs.

THE EDUCATIONAL RATIONALE FOR
ILLUSTRATIONS

As Tyson and Woodward (1989a) and Woodward and Elliott
(1990) noted, educators in states and school districts may
think they are getting textbooks that meet their curricula or
particular needs. In reality, they are choosing from a small
number of books produced for a national market. However, if
textbooks are barometers of what the "market" wants, then
clearly educators want illustrations in textbooks. The process
of selecting textbooks reinforces the market consensus regarding illustrations. Checklists and rating sheets used to
evaluate textbooks prior to selection always feature illustrations as an important evaluation criterion. In a recent study

of instruments used in selecting elementary social studies textbooks, Woodward (1990) found that illustrations were a dominant criterion used in the selection process.

In addition to the fact that selectors seem to be impressed by illustrations in textbooks, educators and publishers often assert that illustrations are an essential element in motivating students to learn. These notions are not very well formulated or based on any research findings. Rather, the argument derives from what appears to excite and motivate students (see Woodward, 1989a). Because students find the flash, color, movement, and intensity of television, computers, and video so entrancing, it follows that textbooks need to mimic these media. Hence, textbooks that have attractive covers, four-color, full-page photographs, and photographs and other illustrations on almost every page are considered to have a better chance of capturing a student's interest than textbooks with fewer illustrations.

A related aspect of this rationale is the belief that students are reluctant learners. It is thought that present day students do not want to learn and cannot learn without the support of illustrations. In other words, whereas bountifully illustrated textbooks try to have the "look" of objects that define a culture students relate to, the illustrations themselves help students move from one page to another. Indeed, one publisher has made the argument to the author that if "picture books" are what it takes to get students to learn, then picture books are what should be produced. Do illustrations motivate students to learn? No evidence from research seems to exist that suggest illustrations motivate students to learn. Publishers claim the importance of illustrations in motivating learning, as do teachers (see Evans et al., 1987). And a few researchers have asserted that pictures have a motivational effect (see Duchastel & Waller, 1979). However, common sense and personal experience would indicate that illustrations, when used judiciously, can serve an instructional and motivational function. The next section investigates the effect of illustrations in textbooks.

ILLUSTRATIONS IN TEXTBOOKS

Market forces exert tremendous influence on the design of textbooks. It follows that if a premium is placed on illustrations, then textbooks will be replete with illustrations. This section investigates the repercussions of the demand for illustrations in textbooks from an instructional viewpoint. Two issues are discussed, first, the amount of space taken up by illustrations compared to expository text, and second, the instructional effectiveness of illustrations.

Illustrations and Expository Text: The Space Crunch

Calls for in-depth content and treatment of topics imply a need for major changes in the way textbooks are selected and designed. Although it may be impossible for textbooks to fully meet the criticism leveled against them, it may be that illustrations and supplementary features take up an inordinate amount of space. In fact, evidence indicates that textbook content, as represented by expository prose, is surprisingly short; thus, if the design elements that surround expository prose are nonessential or do not serve an instructional purpose, then space is being wasted that could otherwise be devoted to expository prose. My (Woodward, 1990) analysis of seven secondary school civics textbooks (copyrights 1980 to 1983) found that these books averaged 545 pages (Table 5.1), with 30% of the average textbook taken up with glossary, index, student activities, unit title pages, and so forth. The remaining pages consisted of "content," defined here as expository prose and illustrations.

What was the result when the space taken up by illustrations was subtracted from the content pages? Much less space was devoted to expository text than at first appeared. Thus, when illustrations were eliminated from content pages, the amount of expository text ranged from 34% to 76%. Of the total, the average textbooks consisted of 545 pages, 389 of which were content pages, 109 pages of which were devoted to illustrations. Only 280 pages (53% of the total textbook pages) were devoted to expository text. When the number of illustrations were compared to the total number of purported content pages, there was one page of illustrations per 1.3 content pages. Although there is a variation in textbooks in the amount of space devoted to expository text, the average civics textbook contains a disappointing proportion of instructional material. We have come

TABLE 5.1

Distribution of Textbook Pages

Textbook	1	2	3	4	5	6	7	Average
Total number textbook pages	575	654	576	439	564	448	560	545
Total pages (proportion) devoted to index glossary, supplementary features	191(.33)	121(.19)	127(.22)	202(.46)	132(.23)	177(.40)	145(.26)	156(.29)
Total pages (proportion) devoted to illustrations	110(.19)	133(.20)	152(.26)	90(.21)	115(.20)	63(.14)	100(.18)	109(.20)
Total pages (proportion) devoted to expository text	274(.48)	400(.61)	297(.52)	147(.33)	317(.56)	208(.46)	315(.56)	280(.51)

TABLE 5.2

Proportion of Illustrations in Two Elementary Science Series

	SERIES A	SERIES B
Grade	Space devoted to illustrations as proportion of content pages	Space devoted to illustrations as proportion of content pages
1	0.79	0.74
2	0.75	0.65
3	0.55	0.47
4	0.48	0.45
5	0.43	0.44
6	0.41	0.43
Average proportion illustrations	0.53	50%

to expect such a textbook to be full of lavish illustrations and supplementary features. Instead of serving a primarily supporting function, these features seem to overwhelm the relatively small amount of expository text in textbooks.

The amount of space devoted to expository prose is not limited to civics textbooks, but seems to be a general problem. For example, an analysis of two recently published elementary (Grade 1 through Grade 6) science series, Woodward (1989b) found that 53% of the chapter content pages in Series A (1985) and 50% in Series B (1985) consisted of illustrations (Table 5.2).[1] As expected, at the lower grade levels, there were more illustrations. Thus, in Series A's first-grade textbook, 79% of the content pages were made up of illustrations; in Grade 2, 75% of the content pages were made up of illustrations. These finding were closely mirrored in Series B. Given that children in the first two grades read with considerable difficulty, picture books may be quite appropriate (although why these children need textbooks is open to question). By the fourth grade, children can usually read with comprehension and this seems to be reflected in

---

[1]Content pages were defined as illustrations and expository text in chapters. They were analyzed, reviewed, and there were assignment pages at the end of each chapter. Index, glossary, unit title pages, illustrations, and so forth, were not analyzed in this study. Page size was measured, as was illustration size, and calculations made to convert illustrations measurements into page equivalents.

the decreasing proportion of pages devoted to illustrations; for example, in the fifth-grade textbook, 43% and 44% for Series A and B respectively contain illustrations. The results of this study are quite startling; textbooks assign approximately the same amount of space to expository text as to illustrations.

The Instructional Effectiveness of Illustrations

Given that illustrations take up a surprisingly large amount of space in textbooks, an important issue is whether these illustrations are instructionally effective. In other words, do they extend knowledge or facilitate students' understanding of particular concepts and topics? In order to find out if illustrations are used effectively, an analysis of the unit/chapters dealing with the topic *electricity* was undertaken. These unit/chapters were taken from the sixth-grade textbooks of the elementary science series previously described. Three factors were analyzed: (a) the use of captions, (b) the instructional effectiveness of illustrations, and (c) whether the textbook's accompanying teacher's guide provided support for using illustrations.

The chapters were divided between those pages that covered content and those that contained an activity or test. The electricity chapter in Series A contained 52 illustrations, representing 36% of total page space; in Series B, 44 illustrations comprised 34% of the content pages of the chapter. There were 10 illustrations in the activity sections of Chapter A and 7 in Chapter B. When activity pages and illustrations were not taken into account, 39% of the content pages in the electricity chapter in Series A and 38% in Series B consisted of illustrations.

Captions. Captions serve a number of important functions; they can provide information as basic as the name of the object, and they can ask a question. Thus, it would seem that the use of captions should be standard policy when designing textbooks.

The following typology was used to characterize the captions:

1. *None.* Illustrations contain no caption.
2. *Title/Name.* Caption identified the object portrayed.

4. *Repeats Text.* Caption repeats or paraphrases the main text.
5. *Extends Text.* Caption contains information about the portrayed object that was not present in the main text.
6. *Questions.* Caption written as a question to the reader.

The use of caption in the two chapters varied quite markedly as can be seen in Table 5.3. For example, 74% of illustrations in Chapter A were accompanied by captions compared with 47% in Chapter B.

Captions were categorized by type, as can be seen in Table 5.4. At the most basic level, captions can simply tell the reader the name of the object portrayed in an illustration. In Chapter A, 29% of captions were titles or names compared to 81% in Chapter B. In a number of cases, titles seemed superfluous—what individual needs to be told that an object is a hairdryer, a food mixer, or a three-pronged outlet? On the other hand, titles can be quite helpful, especially in the case of poorly chosen illustrations or unfamiliar objects; without a caption, a photograph of a single photoelectric cell would remain a mystery.

The link between illustration and content text was stronger when captions paraphrased or repeated content text. For example, a caption read "The electron on each sheet causes the sheets to repel each other," whereas the text noted, "We say that electrons repel each other. The electrons on one sheet were pushed back by the electrons on another." Captions paraphrasing or repeating text content comprised 39% and 19% of the captions for Chapter A and Chapter B respectively.

The science chapter in Series B had no captions that were formulated as questions or provided further information. For

TABLE 5.3
Captions in Electricity Chapters

	Series A	Series B
Number of Illustrations	42	36
Number (proportion) of illustrations with captions	31(.74)	16(.47)

TABLE 5.4
Types of Captions in Electricity Chapters

	Series A	Series B
Number of captioned illustrations:	31	16
Proportion of captions as:		
Titles	0.29	0.81
Repetition of text content	0.39	0.19
Questions to reader	0.19	0
Further information	0.13	0

Chapter A, 19% of the captions were phrased as questions. For example, one caption asked students to apply what they had learned in the text: "How is the electromagnet being used in this scrapyard?" Another asked, "When current flows through the wire, what happens to the nail?" In Series A, 13% of the captions provided additional information that extended the text in some way. For example, an illustration of the Van de Graaff generator was accompanied by a caption, "This Van de Graaff generator can produce between 2 and 3 million volts of electricity."

From an instructional design point of view, creating a strong text-illustration link should facilitate the student's ability to make a strong connection between expository text and pictures, reinforcing content learning. From this vantage point, illustrations should have captions and they should be explicitly mentioned in the text. Thus, a cross-tabulation was constructed to determine the extent to which illustrations were both explicitly mentioned in the text and captioned. This cross-tabulation is shown in Table 5.5. In Chapter A, 31% of illustrations had captions and were mentioned in the text; in Chapter B, only 19% fell into this category. In Chapter A it was more likely for illustrations to be captioned but not mentioned (43%). In the case of Chapter B, it was more likely

TABLE 5.5
Captioning and Mentioning of Illustrations in Electricity Chapters

	Series A		Series B	
	Mention	No Mention	Mention	No Mention
Caption	0.31	0.43	0.19	0.25
No Caption	0.02	0.24	0.39	0.17

Note. Series A, $n = 42$; Series B, $n = 36$.

for illustrations without any accompanying captions to be mentioned in the text (39%). Particularly disturbing from an instructional viewpoint was the large number of illustrations that had no captions *and* were not mentioned in the text. In Chapter A, 24% of illustrations fell into the *no caption/no text mention* category; in Chapter B, 14% of illustrations fell into this category. In these cases, it can be assumed that, either there is no relation between the text and the illustration, or that the student will be required to make an extraordinary effort to draw an inference regarding the relation.

Illustrations.   Given there are numerous illustrations in textbooks, to what extent do they serve an instructional purpose? Clearly, illustrations can still be instructionally useful even if they are not tied to particular text and some, of course, may simply be fillers that are attractive but unrelated to the topic being covered. A typology was developed to reflect the range of functions of illustrations in textbooks. In developing this typology, consideration was given to those previously used by Levin, Anglin, and Carney (1987); and Hunter, Crismore, and Pearson (1987). The typology used in this study was as follows:

1. *Noncontent-related visual.*   No discernible relationship to content; for example, a child playing in a field in a science book.
2. *Tangentially content-related visual.*   An illustration generally related to the topic being covered, but with no direct connection to the text; for example, a picture of a tree in a section on plant growth.
3. *Content supporting visual.*   An illustration offering an example or repetition of text.
4. *Content extending visual.*   An illustration containing additional information that enhances and extends the text.

Illustrations were assigned to the noncontent, tangential, content supporting, or content extending functions. In Chapter A, 22% of illustrations were either noncontent related or tangential to the content, compared to 9% of illustrations in Chapter B (Table 5.6). The lone, noncontent

TABLE 5.6
Relation of Illustrations to Content in Electricity Chapters

	Series A (n = 42)	Series B (n = 36)
	Proportion	
Type of Illustration:		
Unrelated to Content	0.03	—
Tangentially Content Related	0.19	0.09
Content Supporting	0.75	0.86
Content Extending	0.03	0.05

related illustration in Chapter A seemed to be a function of poor layout and design; a photograph of a miniature calculator that had no caption and was (we inferred) supposed to represent a photoelectric cell. Chapter A had the most (19%) of illustrations that were classified as having no direct instructional connection to the text. For example, one illustration consisted of a hand, holding up a piece of twisted wire with the caption, "A metal conductor"—hardly a correct example of conductors. Another illustration showed a solar-powered aircraft. Unfortunately, the text made no connection to the illustration and mentioned no qualities of solar power that would have made the illustration an example that would help a student understand the concept.

The majority of illustrations were related to the text in some way. In Chapter A, 75% of illustrations were related to the text and in Chapter B, 86%. These illustrations were flashes of lightening, circuits, transistors, fuses, and so forth. Only three illustrations from both chapters were judged to extend the text in some way. For example, a photograph of a scrapyard showed a real application for electromagnetism, which was *not* covered in the text. Another illustration showed the range of batteries available and provided a nice contrast between drawings of cells and real life exemplars.

Teachers' Guides and the Instructional Effectiveness of Illustrations. Contemporary textbook series, especially at the elementary and junior high-school levels, consist, not only of the student text, but also of an array of support materials. Teachers' guides are perhaps the most notable of these materials because they contain extensive lesson plans and suggestions for instruction. For example, it is not unusual for a lesson plan to lay out goals and objectives for a lesson, provide an introduction about the topic for the teacher (who can then relay it to his or her students), and then give a running commentary about the lesson itself. Not surprisingly, there is a close correspondence between the teacher's guide and the student textbook. Thus, another element to consider in judging the instructional effectiveness of illustrations is whether the teacher's guide provides suggestions for using illustrations in instruction. Hence, the section of the teacher's guide accompanying the electricity chapter in the two series was analyzed.

In the lesson plan that accompanied the electricity chapter in Series A, illustrations were mentioned in the teacher's guide 17 times; these referred singly and in groupings to 20 out of 42 illustrations. In the case of the electricity chapter in Series B, illustrations were mentioned in the teachers' guide only four times and referred to four illustrations out of 36. Typically, lesson plans would ask teachers to draw students' attention to a particular illustration. For example, "Direct the students attention to the diagrams on the right," and "Ask the students to study the photographs on page___ ."

Although it is hard to make generalizations, it does seem likely that captions, text mention, illustrations related to text, and lesson plan mention are important variables in the instructional effectiveness of illustrations. Given this, what can be said about the instructional effectiveness of illustrations in the two sixth-grade chapters on electricity? From a detailed analysis of the two chapters, much more care had been taken by the publishers of Series A than of Series B in selecting and placing illustrations. In Series A, illustrations were mentioned in text, there were illustrations with captions, captions that provided additional information, teacher's guide mention, and so forth. In the case of Chapter B, illustrations often seemed to be afterthoughts; consequently, in Chapter B, illustrations were generally instructionally ineffective. It could be, as stated, the publisher of Series B did not have an "illustrative strategy." That is, illustrations were simply an important aesthetic feature that did not command much editorial attention during the development of the series.

ILLUSTRATIONS AND RESEARCH

One of the most remarkable things about illustrations in textbooks is that the work of the research community has little impact on either publisher policy or on educators who use illustrations as an important selection criterion. This is in marked contrast to the production and selection of reading basals, where authors and/or consultants are usually noted researchers in the reading field, and consumers have an active professional association with the authors and consultants, which welcomes the insights research brings to the field.

As noted, publishers interviewed by Evans et al. (1987) did not find research on illustrations very relevant; a number of researchers have echoed this sentiment. For example, Houghton and Willows (1987) noted, "At present, it would appear that a great deal of instructional text design is guided by intuition, prior practice, trial and error approaches, and marketability considerations. Correspondingly, much empirical research is conceived of and carried out exclusive of real world contexts that it ultimately seeks to improve" (p. iii). Levie (1987) noted, ". . . research on pictures is not a coherent field of inquiry. . . . Most researchers refer to a narrow range of this literature in devising their hypotheses and in discussing their results" (p. 26). And Peeck (1987) noted that research on illustrations has ignored captions—a particularly unfortunate omission, akin to studying film without listening to the soundtrack.

CONCLUSION

This chapter suggested that the role of illustrations in U.S. elementary and secondary school textbooks is an ambiguous one. A number of factors have compromised the instructional use of illustrations. Concerns about fair representation of women and minorities, the lack of training of those who select textbooks, the concern with noninstructional qualities of textbooks, such as recent copyright date, assumptions about how students learn, and the market for textbooks as perceived by publishers have resulted in confusion as to what standards textbooks should meet. These pressures have produced textbooks in which instructional design and content are considered equally with other myriad concerns, whether they are social, political, or economic.

What seems quite clear is that textbooks are products of a complex market and, although there are many "players" in this market, two principle groups of actors stand out—the selectors or consumers and the producers. This consumer--producer market is one where the actors see little relevance in research, especially as it relates to illustrations, in selecting or producing textbooks. When Evans et al. (1987) interviewed publishers and editors, the publishers said that research was not a factor in determining the number, placement, and function of illustrations. Rather, illustrations were more likely to be determined by marketing considerations, either prompted by teacher feedback or by innovations adopted by competing publishers.

Illustrations are used as a proxy for textbook quality. There are often vague reasonings about illustrations and pupil motivation, but it is more likely that teachers and administrators equate attractive layout and stunning photographs with instructional quality. Unfortunately, there is no necessary connection between bountiful and attractive illustrations and learning. Rather, studies have suggested that many illustrations fail to enhance learning and, in fact, may consume a large portion of limited space that could be better devoted to content. Given that illustrations are used as indicators of quality by selectors, a burden is placed on producers to include vibrant and plentiful illustrations that meet selectors' aesthetic criteria, while, at the same time, ensuring that they are educationally useful. Unfortunately, sometimes publishers do not live up to the challenge; instead, there is evidence that illustrations are hastily assembled, with little regard to their being closely related to the text.

Perhaps most disturbing is the seeming irrelevance of research on illustrations to selectors and producers of textbooks. To date, research has had very little impact and has provided very few guidelines for practical application of illustrations in text. Indeed, the vast majority of research on illustrations is undertaken without regard to actual textbooks or the population that will read them.

It is not clear how the situation can quickly be changed for the better. The market is indeed complex and conservative and is served by a handful of giant publishers, all of whom know what their customers want. So far, there has been no discernible demand for textbooks to include instructionally relevant illustrations. However, before improvement can start, research needs to be done to inform and educate both consumers and producers of textbooks.

ACKNOWLEDGMENT

Special thanks to Lucia French and Adeline Sabol for their assistance with this project.

REFERENCES

Duchastel, P. C., & Waller, R. (1979, November). Pictorial illustration in instructional texts. *Educational Technology*, pp. 20–25.

Evans, M. E., Watson, C., & Willows, D. M. (1987). A naturalistic inquiry into illustrations in instructional textbooks. In H. A. Houghton & D. M. Willows (Eds.), *The psychology of illustration, Vol. 2, Instructional issues.* New York: Springer-Verlag.

Houghton, H. A., & Willows, D. M. (Eds.). (1987). *The psychology of illustration, Vol. 2, Instructional issues.* New York: Springer-Verlag.

Hunter, B., Crismore, A., & Pearson, P. D. (1987). Visual displays in basal readers and social studies textbooks. In H. A. Houghton & D. M. Willows (Eds.), *The psychology of illustration, Vol. 2, Instructional issues.* New York: Springer-Verlag.

Levie, W. H. (1987). Research on pictures: Guide to the literature. In D. M. Willows & H. A. Houghton (Eds.), *The psychology of illustration, Vol. 1, Basic research.* New York: Springer-Verlag.

Levin, J. R., Anglin, G. J., & Carney, R. N. (1987). On empirically validating pictures in Prose. In D. M. Willows & H. A. Houghton (Eds.), *The psychology of illustration, Vol. 1, Basic research.* New York: Springer-Verlag.

O'Brien, S. (1988). The reshaping of history. Marketers vs. authors. *Curriculum Review, 28*(1), 11–14.

Peeck, J. (1987). The role of illustrations in processing and remembering illustrated text. In D. M. Willows & H. A. Houghton (Eds.), *The psychology of illustration, Vol. 1, Basic research.* New York: Springer-Verlag.

Ravitch, D. (1987). Tot sociology: Or what happened to history in the grade schools? *American Scholar, 56,* 343–354.

Sewall, G. T. (1988). American history textbooks: Where do we go from here? *Phi Delta Kappan, 69,* 552–558.

Tyson, H., & Woodward, A. (1989a). Why students aren't learning very much from textbooks. *Educational Leadership, 47*(3), 14–17.

Tyson, H., & Woodward, A. (1989b). Nineteenth century policies for 21st century practice: The textbook reform dilema. *Educational Policy, 3*(2), 95–106.

Woodward, A. (1987). Textbooks: Less than meets the eye. *Journal of Curriculum Studies, 19*(6), 511–526.

Woodward, A. (1989a). Learning by pictures: Comments on learning, literacy, and culture. *Social Education, 53*(2), 101–102.

Woodward, A. (1989b, March). *When a picture isn't worth a thousand words: An analysis of illustrations and content in elementary school science textbooks.* Paper presented at the annual meeting of the American Educational Research Association, San Francisco, CA.

Woodward, A. (1990, April). *Selecting elementary social studies textbooks: A case of forms without substance.* Paper presented at the annual meeting of the American Educational Research Association, Boston, MA.

Woodward, A., & Elliott, D. L. (1990). Textbooks, consensus, and controversy. In D. L. Elliott & A. Woodward (Eds.) *Textbooks and schooling in the United States* (89th Yearbook, Part 1, of the National Society for the Study of Education). Chicago, IL: National Society for the Study of Education.

Woodward, A., & Nagel, K. C. (1987–1988). Old wine in new bottles: An analysis of changes in elementary social studies textbooks from old to new editions. *Book Research Quarterly, 3*(4), 22–33.

—■ 6 ■—
Auxiliary Materials that Accompany Textbooks: Can They Promote "Higher-Order" Learning?

Linda M. Anderson
Michigan State University

Recent calls for educational reform have often centered on students' needs to "learn to think" (Resnick, 1987). Proponents of such reforms argue that it is not enough to teach basic skills, but that students should leave school with meaningful understanding of academic content and the capacity to engage in critical thinking, problem solving, and creative efforts about that content; these goals are subsumed under the currently popular heading of "higher-order" learning or thinking.

This chapter examines recent developments in instructional theory about how so-called higher-order learning is achieved. The chapter argues that the design and use of auxiliary materials that accompany textbooks should reflect contemporary thinking about instruction that promotes rich understanding and thinking about academic content. Auxiliary materials include any written materials that are intended to accompany a textbook; they are often used by teachers as the basis of academic tasks to be carried out by students as they learn content. This includes workbooks, worksheets, and the auxiliary materials that are part of the text itself, such as math problems and the questions and project ideas at the end of chapters, for instance, in social studies or science texts.

ORGANIZATION

Theory about learning and instruction presented first explains higher-order learning and thinking in terms of the contextualization of knowledge. Second, instructional theory that is based on a contextual view of knowledge is described and illustrated with examples from reading and science instruction. Third, principles are derived from the instructional theory and used as the basis for recommendations for the design and use of auxiliary materials.

What is "Higher-Order" Learning?

Higher-order as an adjective that describes learning or thinking has seen widespread use recently. As most people use the term, the category includes such mental acts as critical thinking, problem solving, and creative efforts. The use of the term creates some conceptual problems because it implies that there is also "lower-order" learning and thinking. Moreover, the use of the terms "higher" and "lower" implies that there is a natural hierarchy of knowledge, in which lower-order learning must be acquired before higher learning or thinking is possible.

This sequential, hierarchical view of learning and thinking has both similarities and differences with contemporary instructional theory. The two perspectives are similar in recognizing that in any given situation, some thinking is more adaptive and useful than other thinking. Proponents of both a sequential, hierarchical view and more contemporary instructional theory would argue that there are important differences in how people use their knowledge, and schools should foster more adaptive use of knowledge through critical thinking, problem solving, and creative efforts. However, the two perspectives differ with regard to how schools can best accomplish this.

Contemporary instructional theory posits that students are more adaptive users of their own knowledge when that knowledge is contextually rich. In contrast, when knowledge is contextually limited, it is less likely to be available for critical thinking, problem solving, and creative efforts. In both situations, skills, facts, vocabulary, and procedural rules (often considered "lower-order" learning) are present. The difference is how those skills, facts, vocabulary, and procedural rules are related to other knowledge.

In many ways, the acquisition and use of contextually rich knowledge parallels most people's understanding of the outcomes of so-called higher-order thinking and learning, and the use and acquisition of contextually limited knowledge parallels common understandings about the results of so-called lower-order thinking and learning.

The two sets of terms are not meant to be synonymous, however, because the theoretical assumptions that underlie them are very different. Contemporary theorists, who emphasize the context of knowledge, disagree with the assumption that there is a necessary hierarchy of learning, in which some content (lower-order learning) must be acquired before higher-order thinking can occur. Contemporary theorists argue instead that prerequisites for critical thinking, problem solving, and creative efforts can not be defined in terms of specific content, but rather must be defined in terms of the individual learner's understanding of that content—whether and how the individual's knowledge of that content is embedded in a context that makes certain information retrievable in new situations.

Knowledge in Context: Contemporary Instructional Theory

The contemporary instructional theory described in this chapter is based on ideas about the social construction (and continual reconstruction) of knowledge. Knowledge is the "stuff" of mental life: the concepts, propositions, procedures, and beliefs that an individual or a community uses as the basis for perceiving, thinking about, remembering, and learning about the world.

Knowledge is organized into structures or networks that relate various concepts, propositions, procedures, and beliefs. This organization is actively constructed by the knower (an individual or a community such as scholars in a discipline) by relating new information to prior knowledge. That is, all new learning results from the relating of something unfamiliar to something that is already known. Thus, what a person or a community knows is not a "basket of facts" but rather is a complexly interrelated conceptual network that is always changing with new experience (Anderson, 1984; Glaser, 1984; Resnick, 1987).

This conceptual network provides the context within which any particular piece of knowledge is embedded. All knowledge is contextualized, but some knowledge is embedded in a richer context than other knowledge.

For example, consider a case of mathematics learning described by Hiebert and Lefevre (1986). They described the importance of connecting procedural knowledge (how to get correct solutions to math problems) with conceptual knowledge (the meanings of the symbols and operations, and understanding why the procedures make sense). In this example, they contrast contextually limited knowledge of how to add decimals with contextually rich knowledge. They show how remembering and using the knowledge in problem solving is more likely in the contextually rich case:

> Suppose students are learning to add decimal numbers and the teacher says, "When you add decimals you must first line up the decimal points." If this is all the information students acquire about setting up decimal addition problems, the line-up-the-decimal-points rule likely will be stored as an isolated piece of information [i.e., contextually limited knowledge] with retrieval dependent on retracing a single link between the procedure and the perception of an addition problem as one involving decimal numbers. However, if students also learn that the concept underlying the procedure is the adding together of things that are alike, and they are able to recognize the similarity between this rationale and that used in adding whole numbers or common fractions [i.e., they have contextually rich knowledge], they are in a much better position to remember the rule. The likelihood of recalling the appropriate procedure can be accessed by crossing a number of different conceptual bridges (e.g., ideas about place value or about common denominators, or intuitive notions about relative sizes of quantities). In fact, with this sort of conceptual base, the rule could be reconstructed extemporaneously. (p. 11)

As this example demonstrates, a contextually rich knowledge structure is one in which there are many concepts that are connected to one another in many different ways. The conceptual connections include, for example, cause–effect explanations, rule–example sets, and sequences. When a person holds contextually rich knowledge, knowledge structures about different topics are united through relationships that specify common underlying principles (as was the case in the example given, where the common principle is that you can only add quantities whose units are alike).

Perhaps most important, when knowledge is contextually rich, the knowledge about a topic is related to the situations or types of problems to which that knowledge is applicable. That is, the knower may have an explicit understanding about how, why, and when knowledge can be applied and used. The knower is therefore more capable of defining the nature of problems and deciding on possible solutions.

As Hiebert and Lefevre (1986) pointed out, contextually rich knowledge is more easily accessed than contextually limited knowledge. Access to knowledge occurs through conceptual relationships, which act as paths along which reasoning may travel from idea to idea. When there are multiple connections among pieces of knowledge about a topic (the situation that defines contextual richness), then there are more ways to reach and use any particular piece of knowledge. When one has learned something (such as the procedure for adding decimals) in a very limited way, relating it only to certain situations (e.g., math problems in the book), then one has fewer routes to finding relevant knowledge during a novel problem situation.

Learning academic content in school can result in contextually rich knowledge or it may result in contextually limited knowledge. When the former occurs, students are more likely to use their knowledge of the content in ways that teachers, parents, and employers find gratifying and "smart" and they may label it "higher-order" thinking. When the latter occurs, those same teachers, parents and employers shudder at the inadequacies of our educational system, and call for reforms to teach more thinking skills or problem solving.

Criticizing Textbooks and Auxiliary Materials in Light of Contemporary Instructional Theories. Several criticisms have been leveled against textbooks and auxiliary materials, faulting them for a lack of conceptual cohesion and a focus on discrete, disconnected facts and skills (Beck & McKeown, 1988; Durkin, 1987; Osborn, 1984; Roth & Anderson, 1988; Tyson-Bernstein, 1988). Such criticisms suggest that many textbooks and auxiliary materials are used in a way (perhaps can *only* be used in a way) that promotes contextually limited knowledge. When working with the tasks set forth by textbooks and auxiliary materials, students learn to give responses to specific cues, such as questions phrased a certain way or problems expressed in a certain form. Students are seldom encouraged to go beyond the particular questions or problems posed by the materials in order to build a richer context for their content learning.

Many textbooks and their auxiliary materials appear to be based on a theory of learning that considers content and its sequencing the most important determinant of learning. Thus, students are asked to recall content or to apply procedures to demonstrate that they can reproduce the content in a form that is considered correct. Then, more content is presented that logically (in the eyes of the textbook writer) builds on the preceding content.

What is missing from this perspective is a focus on the ways that learners are making sense of the content they are encountering. Fostering the learner's efforts to put that content into a larger context is not the critical, driving purpose of many texts and auxiliary materials. Thus, the design and use of most auxiliary materials is not congruent with contemporary instructional theory about how to promote critical thinking, problem solving, and creative efforts.

What Do We Know About Instruction That Promotes Contextually Rich Knowledge?

The broad outlines of a theory of knowledge and its construction were just presented. What then is known about the kinds of instruction that promote more contextually rich knowledge? Is there a place in that instruction for auxiliary materials that accompany textbooks?

In order to address those questions, examples of reading and science instruction are presented. For each subject, there are contrasting cases of instruction that appear to promote contextually rich knowledge or contextually limited knowledge. Following the examples, the features of instruction that appear to promote contextually rich knowledge are considered for their applicability to the design and use of auxiliary materials.

Examples From Reading Instruction. The content taught in these examples is "finding the main idea" when reading, an item that appears on numerous school districts' lists of curriculum objectives. Few would argue that being able to find (and communicate) main ideas is a useful skill. If we were unable to extract the gist of a text, we would be unable to separate critical features of an idea from supporting details when remembering or communicating it.

In many classrooms, finding the main idea is identified by the basal reading program as a distinct skill. Students receive practice in finding the main idea with auxiliary materials that accompany the basals. Within these materials, a common kind of task is to read a passage, and then to choose one of three or four candidates for the "main idea" of the passage. The passages presented are ones in which the main idea is clear and the choices are laid out for the child. Once the work is completed, it is graded by the teacher, sometimes along with a discussion of why answers are right or wrong, sometimes with no discussion.

Consider what knowledge is constructed by an elementary student about how to find the main idea when his only explicit instruction in this skill is in the context of the basal text and accompanying materials. First of all, he learns that "find the main idea" is a task tied to instructional materials. That is, it is schoolwork, and knowledge about how to find main ideas is useful mainly when completing schoolwork. Even within the limited context of schoolwork, this skill is to be used only when a particular stimulus is given (i.e., the question, "Find the main idea"). There is one correct answer, always, with no room for disagreement among students for different interpretations of the passage or for adjustments in main idea as the paragraphs add up to a longer story or essay. Furthermore, that one correct answer is usually given in the task itself, not generated by the student himself except on rare, open-ended questions. Even then, the passages to be read are usually written so that the main idea is not very ambiguous.

In the early elementary grades, tasks of this sort dominate

the auxiliary materials. The knowledge thus constructed by an elementary student about how to find the main idea is contextually limited to the situation defined by workbook activities of a certain kind. For lower-achieving students who do not receive additional literacy experiences, the tasks set by typical auxiliary materials contribute to beliefs and strategic knowledge that are not supportive of higher-order thinking (Anderson, Brubaker, Alleman-Brooks, & Duffy, 1985).

The reading workbook context is not very much like other school (or life) situations in which written text is a tool for learning content and in which identification of main ideas serves a purpose other than completing a workbook page. For example, the student might read a book and then want to report to others about the book (not an uncommon school assignment). Successfully communicating with others about something that one has read requires, first of all, defining the situation as one in which the main idea should be identified and summarized. Such situational definition is seldom a part of the tasks posed by auxiliary materials.

Then, the student must analyze the text (which is usually longer than what is presented in the auxiliary materials). The student must then create the main idea, because multiple-choice options are not presented. He or she may need to realize that the main idea is sometimes not clear or that there may be multiple main ideas, any of which is refined as the book progresses.

Finally, the student cannot stop once a main idea has been identified because the purpose of the task is to use that main idea for some purpose (such as communicating to others about a book; the main idea gives some common ground upon which one's evaluation could be based). Therefore, the student must monitor the successfulness of his or her attempts to explain main ideas by gauging listeners' understanding and adjusting as necessary (by filling in additional details that make clearer what the book was mainly about).

In order to successfully carry out the application of knowledge about how to find the main idea, then, one needs to have richly contextualized knowledge about: (a) when and why finding and expressing the main idea is useful (i.e., what are situations in which one should find the main idea); (b) how alternative interpretations may be possible and how and when to choose among them; and (c) how to determine whether the communication of the main idea is serving the intended purpose. Such knowledge does not result when a student's experience is limited to the tasks posed by auxiliary materials of the sort described.

In contrast, consider two alternative ways of teaching about finding main ideas when reading. The first example is Reciprocal Teaching, a method for teaching about reading comprehension that has had positive results in a variety of studies (Palincsar & Brown, 1984, 1989). In Reciprocal Teaching, comprehension-monitoring and comprehension-fostering skills are developed by students as they participate within a group. All students read passages silently (or, with younger students, listen to them read aloud), and then the teacher or a student responds to the passage by asking questions about main ideas, summarizing, clarifying, and predicting future content. The purpose of the activity is not to get correct answers, but rather to provide practice in thinking about the questions that fluent readers ask themselves to promote reading comprehension. The teacher initially models how to respond to a passage and provides coaching to students as they begin to respond, but as time goes on, the students take over the teacher's role and discuss the passages with each other.

In this example, the knowledge about reading comprehension that is constructed by the students includes many of the elements missing from the first example offered. The students learn that mental responses to text occur in more contexts than workbook activities. They learn that there are few singly correct answers to such tasks as summarizing or asking questions about the main idea. Because the text material used for practice of comprehension is content-area text, they learn that the new skills they are acquiring apply to more than basal reading materials and their accompanying workbooks. Thus, their knowledge is not so contextually limited as it would be if learning only occurred through practice on workbook activities.

The second reading example does involve the use of auxiliary materials for teaching about reading comprehension. The materials were developed by Scheu, Tanner, and Au (1988) for use with native Hawaiian students who had a history of low school achievement.

In response to their own frustration with auxiliary materials that accompanied the basal readers, Scheu et al. developed a variety of alternative worksheet formats to support their comprehension-based reading program. Students read stories from commercial basals, but most of their supporting independent work came from teacher-developed worksheets, not the commercial workbooks.

In an example described in Scheu et al. (1988), before reading a story about a hippopotamus in a jungle, the students composed sentences expressing their prior knowledge about jungles. The teacher then used their answers as the basis of a dialogue about their prior knowledge, and as they talked, she drew a semantic map to show relationships among their ideas. (Similar suggestions for design of pre-reading auxiliary materials are offered by Cunningham, 1984.) Through the use of this activity, the knowledge that would be useful in comprehending the upcoming story (i.e., the context within which learning from the story would occur) is activated and enriched.

After each segment of the story was read, the students did an independent assignment related to the main idea of that segment, ending with worksheets on which they mapped this particular story onto a problem-solution story structure, a concept that the teacher had been emphasizing for several weeks and representing to the students with each story they read. (Thus, finding the main idea is not limited to analysis of single paragraphs, but is extended to entire stories and the patterns they follow.)

Each time the students completed a worksheet or other activity related to the basal story, the next reading group began with a discussion of what students had thought about, why they had answered as they did, and how ideas were related. For example, the teacher returned to the original semantic map to enrich it in a further discussion, making explicit to students how knowledge gained from reading the story was imbedded in the context of the prior knowledge they had before reading.

Prominently featured throughout the lesson, especially when a new worksheet was assigned, were questions and answers about purposes for the written assignments (e.g., "These are the most important words in the story and we are practicing using them to read the story better").

Throughout the students' work with the auxiliary materials that accompanied the story, the theme of understanding the story and relating it to other knowledge was continually emphasized. The students therefore had the opportunity to see that the activity of identifying main ideas (in the form of a larger structure than single paragraphs) is part of coming to understand a story and seeing its connection to their own lives.

Examples From Science Instruction. Far too many students learn from science textbooks that answers to science questions can be found by attending to the words in boldface type or by memorizing definitions. The end-of-the-chapter questions (the auxiliary materials in the case of many science texts) may lead students to develop strategies of overreliance on details and terms without attempting to link those details together into a contextually rich knowledge structure.

For example, Roth and Anderson (1988) described one seventh grader (of above-average reading achievement) who focused her reading about photosynthesis on the big new words:

> When asked to tell what she had read about, Tracey described the book as being about particular words or phrases ("It was about chlor-something and an ecosystem.") She could not attach any meaning to these words or relate the words to each other. In spite of this lack of attention to meaning, she felt she understood the text [only expressing confusion] when she came to words that were difficult for her to decode (e.g., chlorophyll).

> [When Tracey answered the questions found in the text], her strategy . . . was to look for the big word in the question, find the big word in the text, and copy the surrounding words or sentence. Using this strategy, she was able to answer many of the text-posed questions accurately. [For the question, "What is photosynthesis?], Tracey wrote, "Photosynthesis is a food-making process." But when asked to reread a paragraph that defined photosynthesis and to then describe photosynthesis, Tracey did not have any meaning for the word. She described photosynthesis vaguely as "some kind of chemical or name or something." [At the end of the unit of study, when asked], "Can you tell me anything about photosynthesis?, Tracey

replied, "No, I don't remember it saying anything about it."
Thus, the question–answering process had been meaningless
for Tracey in the sense of developing an understanding of the
text content. It *was* meaningful to her, however, because it
enabled her to complete a school task successfully.

When asked what she knew about how a real plant sitting in
the classroom got its food, Tracey relied totally on [the ideas
she had before reading the text, which were incompatible with
the scientific explanation.] Tracey used her knowledge about
schooling and science classrooms to make sense of the textbook without ever recognizing that it conflicted with her
real-world thinking about plants. (p. 115)

Tracey's knowledge of photosynthesis was quite contextually limited; it was only used when she had to complete
written questions from the text in the presence of the text.
Although not all students exhibit the lack of understanding
shown by Tracey, it is not untypical for students to progress
through science instruction without developing contextually
rich knowledge that they can apply to explaining, predicting,
and controlling real-world phenomena (Anderson & Roth,
1989).

In contrast, consider this example of science teaching from
Kathleen Roth (personal communication, March 16, 1989).
Thirty fifth-grade students were learning about ecosystems,
building upon their previous study of photosynthesis and
animal body systems. On the day observed, attention was
focused on the sealed class aquarium, which had been set up
as an intact ecosystem, so that the fish and other animals
survived on the basis of the plants' production of food and
oxygen through photosynthesis. The teacher wanted the
students to understand that the only necessary input into
this or any other ecosystem is light energy, which is con-
verted by the plants into food energy; which is consumed by
the animals who use food energy to live and reproduce, and
who eventually die and decay so that their minerals are
returned to the soil for use by the plants, who continue to
make food that is eaten by the new generation, and so forth.
If light energy continues, and if there has been an initial
balance of organisms and chemicals in the ecosystem, and if
nothing is done to upset this balance, then the system will
sustain itself. (This idea was one of the goals for the whole
unit; it was not the objective for this lesson only.)

Two activities preceded the use of auxiliary materials. First, students held a discussion with make-believe potato plant (portrayed by the teacher), discussing what was similar about the potato plant and her cousin, the water plant. Second, students role played the actions that occur in photosynthesis, with students acting as light energy, carbon dioxide, and so forth. Then, the students were given a seatwork task to do. It is noteworthy that both of the preceding activities were selected to activate the students' prior knowledge that would be relevant to reasoning through the seatwork task.

The auxiliary material used to define the task was a chart to be completed. It began with a place to list "Populations in our aquarium ecosystem" and, for each population (such as guppies, water plants, snails), there were columns headed by these questions: "What do they need to live?" "How will they get it in this system?" and "Does it have to be added from outside?" "Why?" These questions could not be answered through straight recall, nor could the answers be found verbatim in a textbook. The answers had to be constructed by the students, based on their prior knowledge (from earlier instruction) and their observations of the aquarium.

The last questions on the chart ("Does it have to be added? Why?") were the most critical as far as the main idea of the unit was concerned. However, the other questions served to guide the students' thinking to the conclusion that only light energy was needed from outside the ecosystem.

The charts were done by pairs of students who were accustomed to working with each other. They each discussed the questions, then agreed upon what to write. The discussions were focused on the necessary reasoning and questioning, and sometimes led to seeking further information. For example, one pair of girls asked the teacher, "Won't the air and carbon dioxide and oxygen run out eventually?" This question (and their comments) showed that they realized that the plants and animals could produce the needed gases for each other at least initially, but they were uncertain how long this would work. Engagement with this task led them to raise a question that puzzled them and that represented a key idea in the unit.

The teacher, knowing that this question would be discussed at length later in the unit, when the concept of matter cycling would be introduced, told them to write the question at the bottom of their sheet in the space designated for students' questions. If she had provided the "correct" answer at that time—that the substances would not run out in a balanced ecosystem—they might have simply completed their charts and ceased to wonder about their question. Instead, by delaying an answer, the teacher could respond at a later time when there was a better chance to help the students reason through the question. In this class, the role of worksheets such as this chart was not to collect correct answers but rather to serve as an expression of the students' thinking and questions.

As the student pairs talked and wrote, the teacher circulated, often telling a pair that they needed to add a reason for an answer. This request was not made only for incorrect answers; it reflected a norm in the class that reasoning should be explained, and that *yes* or *no* answers were almost always insufficient.

This paper was turned in and the teacher examined the students' answers to determine whether and how they were applying their knowledge of topics studied earlier to the problem of explaining how the ecosystem worked. On other occasions, assignments like this were followed by class discussion, in which students compared their conclusions with one another. For example, the following day, the teacher assigned a paper that showed a picture of a pond with fish and plants and posed a problem: "When the pond froze and was covered with snow, the organisms died. The next winter, the farmer swept the snow off the ice, and the organisms did not die even though the winter was just as cold. Why?" After the students had completed this page, they discussed their answers and concluded (with guidance from the teacher) that the sun coming into the pond was sufficient to sustain life. This conclusion supported the main idea that the teacher wanted the students to understand well—that within ecosystems, only sunlight is needed from outside in order to sustain life.

By the end of the unit, students appeared to understand this main idea and could explain and reason about several aspects of ecosystems, including food chains, energy flow, chemical changes in matter, and conservation of matter. Their knowledge of one component, such as photosynthesis, was contextually rich, in that it was connected to several other concepts, so that the mechanisms and the purposes of photosynthesis were understood in terms of its role in ecosystems. This contrasts sharply to the contextually limited knowledge of students like Tracey, who learned about photosynthesis only in terms of the textbook's factual presentation and questions.

Characteristics of Instruction That Help Students Construct Contextually Rich Knowledge: Implications for the Design and Use of Auxiliary Materials

Three previous examples were given of instruction that helped students develop contextually rich knowledge. These examples are similar to other examples of instruction that appears to promote meaningful understanding of content and independent problem solving and reasoning (e.g., see Englert & Raphael, 1989; Lampert, 1986; Scardamalia & Bereiter, 1985; Schoenfeld, 1985).

The three examples were contrasted to the use of typical auxiliary materials that resulted in contextually limited knowledge. If there are problems with the ways that auxiliary materials are typically used, then what are the implications of recent instructional theory for alternatives to the typical design and use of auxiliary materials?

Three implications are offered here. These are grounded in emerging theories of instruction that are presented in greater detail elsewhere (Bereiter & Scardamalia, 1985; Collins, Brown, & Newman, 1989; Palincsar, 1986; Perkins & Salomon, 1989; Resnick, 1987; Wertsch, 1979). The implications are offered for the design of tasks which could be reflected in auxiliary materials to textbooks.

Tasks That Lead to Contextually Rich Knowledge Through Scaffolding. The purpose of most academic tasks should be to engage students in the construction of increasingly richer contexts for their knowledge. Such tasks should be of moderate difficulty, requiring some assistance through "scaffolding" provided by the teacher or built into the task materials.

That is, academic tasks should help students to form new connections between ideas, and thus, to create richer contexts for knowledge about particular facts or skills. Especially important are connections that help students understand "how" and "why" relationships. Therefore, tasks should engage students in formulating those relationships and in using knowledge about those relationships to solve problems. The source for many problems should be the "real" physical or social world. Problems may include explaining natural phenomenon, predicting events, or deciding on action.

In the two aforementioned reading examples, students did not receive practice in finding the main idea for its own sake. They engaged in the tasks assigned to them in order to enrich their understanding of the stories or textbooks they were reading. The problem they were solving was determining interpretations of written text. "Finding the main idea" was a tool that was useful for building understanding *about* the text.

In the science example, the use of the worksheet helped the students to track their reasoning about the content of the unit. The problem in the science example was explaining and predicting natural phenomena. The task focused them on a critical question ("What needs to be added from the outside of the aquarium?"), which helped them construct a richer understanding of ecosystems and the place of photosynthesis within them.

In all three cases, an additional purpose was served for the teacher: She gained insight into the students' thinking and could adjust instruction accordingly. These tasks required students to reveal their thinking and reasoning, not just their judgments about correct answers, and therefore, yielded greater insight for the teacher than the students' short responses to typical workbook exercises or factual questions at the end of the chapter.

In order to help students to purposefully reason through a problem, the tasks each were characterized by "scaffolding" built into them. *Scaffolding* is a term used in much recent instructional research to describe the conceptual support given to a learner as she thinks through a problem. Ideally, most tasks are of moderate difficulty for learners, matching their "zone of proximal development" (Cole, 1985; Vygotsky, 1978). This zone is the difference between what a learner can accomplish with no assistance and what a learner can accomplish with some assistance.

When learners only receive tasks that they can accomplish with no assistance, they are not likely to construct richer contexts for their knowledge. Instead, they are routinely applying what they already know well. (Sometimes such routine application practice may be useful; the argument here is that it accomplishes other goals than the construction of contextually rich knowledge.)

In contrast, when learners only attempt tasks that are too difficult, even with assistance, they will not be able to construct new knowledge because they will be unable to link new information to their prior knowledge. For example, imagine trying to teach calculus to a 7-year-old. Even with assistance, the child is unlikely to be able to reason through the problem because the basic concepts do not match anything familiar to the child.

Thus, the ideal level of task difficulty when the purpose is to enrich one's knowledge is the zone of proximal development: the area where the learner is capable of reasoning and seeing new connections, given some assistance from a more knowledgeable peer or adult. Through social interactions with this more knowledgeable person, the learner is guided through the task, making the decisions or receiving modeling and feedback about how to make decisions. (The example of Reciprocal Teaching of reading and listening comprehension that was described earlier is based directly on this instructional theory.) Recent research suggests that these sorts of interactions are the basis of the development of independent reasoning skills or "self-regulation" of cognition (Wertsch, 1979).

However, this theory leaves teachers with a dilemma if they interpret it to mean that no valuable learning can occur unless the learner is engaged in intensive dialogue about a problem. In a classroom of 30 students, it is very difficult to provide constant interactional support. Fortunately, the advantages of scaffolded instruction are not limited to verbal, face-to-face modes. Scaffolding can be built into written tasks if there is sufficient knowledge by the teacher about what kinds of conceptual support will be needed by the students.

For example, in the Scheu et al. (1988) example of seatwork, there was scaffolding built into the sequencing of worksheets done for a single story. The students built up an understanding of the story structure gradually through the questions that they were asked across the week. The questions, by directing the students' attention to the relevant aspects of the story, served as scaffolding along the way to constructing a complete notion of the story's main themes.

Similarly, in the science example, the chart about ecosystems contained questions that helped the students activate their prior knowledge that would help them answer the critical question about what needed to be added to the ecosystem. If the worksheet only included the final, critical question, fewer students would have been able to reach a conclusion. However, by asking the intermediate questions of "What is needed by this population?" and "Where will this population get what it needs to live?" the worksheet helped students sort out what they already knew and could use to reason about the final question.

Thus, tasks that have the purpose of helping to develop contextually rich knowledge should be aimed at the students' "zone of proximal development," creating problems that are difficult without assistance but possible with that assistance. When the problems can not be attempted in the presence of a teacher, then auxiliary materials can provide some of the necessary scaffolding by building in the guiding questions that help students reason their way through the problem. As students demonstrate that they are building rich understandings, the degree of scaffolding built into the tasks should be reduced so that students can practice more independent problem solving with that particular set of ideas. Of course, as new, more complex ideas are introduced, the higher level of scaffolding would be reinstated (Collins et al., 1989).

Tasks That Provide Multiple Representations of Significant Ideas. Significant ideas (such as ways of finding and using main ideas when reading, or the role of light energy in ecosystems), become richly contextualized only when they are encountered in a variety of situations, and their applicability is seen in many different kinds of problems. Otherwise, there is a danger that the student will have only contextually limited knowledge about the idea, such as Tracey, who only encountered photosynthesis as a word to be used in answering science questions, not an idea that could help her understand the natural world.

In the previous examples, there were multiple representations of the significant ideas through a variety of problems and situations. For the reading example, the students engaged in the task of comprehending content through analysis of story structure for almost every basal story or tradebook that they read. For the science example, numerous problems were presented to the students about food chains and the role of light energy. The teacher commented that, although it may have seemed to an observer that she was covering "the same old ground" each new task presented a challenge to students in that they had to apply their knowledge in a slightly different way than before (Kathleen Roth, personal communication, April, 1989).

When multiple representations are used, it is important that students be assisted to see what is the same about all of the situations. ("This is another example of how critical sunlight is to ecosystems, just like the example of. . . .") Understanding the general principles that link different problems or situations is a critical part of building rich contexts for knowledge (Perkins & Salomon, 1989).

Tasks Within Social Settings That Facilitate Dialogues. Tasks should be done within a social setting that allows dialogue with peers and with the teacher about the students' thinking about the tasks. When students are learning about something that is new to them, dialogue with other students and with the teacher about the content is essential for the construction of richly contextualized knowledge. Dialogue is more than a straightforward recitation of answers in response to teachers' factual questions. It involves extended discussion of ideas, with elaboration to explain and to follow through lines of thinking (Palincsar, 1986).

In the aforementioned examples, tasks were the basis for dialogue. The Reciprocal Teaching method is most clearly an example of this, in that it is based entirely on teacher–student and student–student dialogue. However, even when tasks were originally assigned as written work to be done away from the teacher, they still served as the basis for dialogue. In the Scheu et al. (1988) reading example, the students always talked about their written work with the teacher and the group, and this often resulted in story structures or semantic maps that were used throughout the rest of the week.

In the science example, the students engaged in dialogue with each other as a part of doing one task. The joint construction of answers and questions often leads to more sophisticated thinking than individuals are capable of alone. When the purpose of tasks is to engage students in thinking (rather than evaluating them for what they know), then working together supports that purpose (Brown & Palincsar, 1989).

The science teacher spent a great deal of her time in dialogue with students about tasks. During their seatwork time, she talked with individuals about their answers, and sometimes pushed them to explain their reasoning further; she often provided additional scaffolding by asking a question or providing information to help someone think through a problem. After the completion of tasks, she sometimes conducted whole-class dialogues, in which students would offer their answers, sometimes disagreeing with each other and discussing the differences. These large group discussions then provided students with opportunities to add to or revise their own thinking, and the teacher often encouraged them to modify their papers if they wanted to change their answers.

In both the reading and science examples, the dialogue that occurred during and after the tasks was critical to learning from the task. If students had simply completed papers and turned them in, receiving only a grade or written comments, they would not have learned as much from these tasks. The dialogue helps to identify and correct misunderstandings and it may lead students to consider additional information that they had not considered when doing the task originally.

Through dialogue, additional scaffolding can be provided to whatever was built into written materials. Because the scaffolding built into materials can only be based on best guesses about what will aid most students, it may not be sufficient for all students. Only the teacher can design alternative scaffolding on the spot to help a student reason through a problem.

CONCLUSIONS ABOUT THE DESIGN AND USE OF AUXILIARY MATERIALS

In many respects, the discussion in this chapter has not focused on existing auxiliary materials per se. That was intentional, because it makes little sense to think about the design and use of materials outside of the larger context of instruction and the academic tasks that are part of it.

However, this larger context makes it difficult to present simple recommendations for the design and use of auxiliary materials. What would be necessary to design and use materials in a manner that reflects the three principles just offered? Clearly, more than the workbooks or end-of-the-chapter questions that accompany textbooks would have to change. Just as clearly, a larger group than textbook publishers must commit to those changes. Teachers, administrators, and parents would also have to seek certain changes in order for textbooks and their auxiliary materials to change significantly. Some of the necessary changes are described here.

Changing Assumptions About Learning and Knowledge

One necessary change, on the part of all involved, would be to question the theoretical basis on which most current auxiliary materials are based. Even though they are seldom made explicit, there are some assumptions about learning and knowledge that underlie the design and use of most textbooks and materials. One assumption is that students learn by engaging with content, and the more engagement they have, the better they will know something regardless of the nature of that engagement.

This assumption ignores most that has been learned in the past two decades about the active, constructive nature of learning, especially the kind of learning that enables critical thinking, problem solving, and creative efforts. Yet, many textbooks are written, and many teachers teach (and many parents expect that teachers will teach) as if learning could be stamped into students through persistent exposure. Such an approach to teaching usually results in contextually limited knowledge.

Another theoretical assumption that underlies much current practice is the idea that complex mental processes (so-called higher-order thinking) can be broken down into lower-order skills and knowledge. This assumption has led to a facts-and-skills orientation to curriculum design, which is reflected in textbooks and auxiliary materials. As described at the beginning of the chapter, this view of learning is not supported by contemporary theories and supporting research about how to promote critical thinking, problem solving, and creative efforts.

Changing Assumptions About Classroom Organization and the Purposes of Tasks

Current textbooks and auxiliary materials are selected because they fit with instruction as it is typically conducted. In this typical picture, tasks are performed for purposes of making the content stick to the student (according to the theoretical view just described) and evaluating students. Tasks are most often to be performed alone, without assistance from other students.

Within this typical picture, there are quite often dedicated, loving teachers and enthusiastic students, so this should not be interpreted as a blanket indictment of the educational system. However, the typical approach to instruction is not succeeding at, and is not likely to succeed at, attaining the goals of equitable access to knowledge that allows critical thinking, problem solving, and creative efforts.

In order to pursue these goals, some of the typical features of classroom organization and uses of tasks will have to change. First, the emphasis on solitary (and sometimes competitive) work must shift to allow for more collaborative small-group work and true dialogue among class members. Perhaps the design of auxiliary materials could help to promote this by posing tasks that might yield several different answers that could be the basis of discussion.

Second, the use of tasks primarily as assessment devices must shift toward the use of tasks as stimuli for the construction of contexts for knowledge. Students' answers should be viewed, not so much as an indication of *whether* they know something, but of *how* they currently know something. Because knowledge is continually being constructed, tasks should be designed to reveal changes in students' thinking. For example, in the science classroom described, discussion that followed written work often resulted in students adding to or changing their papers, because they had changed their minds or learned something new during the discussion.

Writing it down gave them the opportunity to express their new knowledge. Typically, now, in classrooms where tasks serve largely evaluative purposes, such additions would be viewed as cheating, or, at least, corrections, with the original answer counting in the gradebook.

Changes in Supports for Instruction:
Textbooks, Teachers' Guides and Staff Development,
Curriculum Guidelines, and Assessment Criteria

Several factors external to the classroom affect what teachers and students are able to do within it. Before changes in auxiliary materials would effect changes in students' learning, many of those external factors would also have to change. Otherwise, teachers would be without support to implement the kind of instruction that promotes richly contextualized knowledge.

The qualities of textbooks are discussed elsewhere in this volume. Many textbooks are denounced for poor writing, too little depth, and too many topics (Tyson-Bernstein, 1988). Unless students have access to reasonable presentations of information through textbooks, teachers are left responsible for devising meaningful curricula. This is tremendously demanding, and so almost all teachers must rely on texts to some extent. Unless the quality of those texts is improved, then changes in auxiliary materials will have little impact on students' learning.

Teachers have an incredibly complex job, and they deserve all of the support they can get. Unfortunately, they get too little. In order to teach in a manner that supports the development of richly contextualized knowledge, teachers need the attentive support of administrators, over a long time, in which they can try and reflect on changes in instructional practice. Teachers' guides that support the desired changes in practice would be invaluable, but most current teachers' guides simply reinforce the view that the teacher is there to bring passive students in contact with the content that external authorities have decreed is important. Auxiliary materials that adhere to the guidelines offered in this chapter, along with teaching suggestions about how to use the tasks to promote dialogue, would be invaluable assets to teachers who would like to try alternative approaches to instruction.

School districts and state departments of education set policies that shape the nature of the textbooks that are purchased (and the auxiliary materials that are available). These decisions are often based on the curriculum objectives and the evaluation criteria used to justify the educational program (Tyson-Bernstein, 1988). In order to change the nature of the auxiliary materials that shape the tasks with which students spend so much time, it will be necessary for state and district-level policymakers to understand more about the nature of instruction that promotes the higher-order objectives written into the state curriculum guides.

Is There Any Hope?

Several major changes have just been outlined that would be necessary to effect and to make effective any changes in auxiliary materials. The list is daunting. But there is room for optimism as well. A chapter such as this could not have been written even 10 years ago, and the fact that the symposium on which this book is based brought together textbook publishers, practitioners, and theoreticians is a positive sign that many educators are beginning to question how best to design textbooks and auxiliary materials. The examples offered in this chapter (from Scheu et al., 1988, and from Kathleen Roth, personal communications) represent the efforts of teachers and teacher educators to begin the task of reshaping auxiliary materials. Hopefully, such efforts will be sustained and, within the next decade, the educational community will continue to enrich its own knowledge about the role of textbooks, auxiliary materials, and the instructional practices they support.

REFERENCES

Anderson, C. W., & Roth, K. J. (1989). Teaching science for meaningful understanding and self-regulation. In J. Brophy (Ed.), *Advances in research on teaching: Vol 1. Teaching for meaningful understanding and self-regulated learning* (pp. 265–310). Greenwich, CT: JAI.

Anderson, L. M., Brubaker, N., Alleman-Brooks, J., & Duffy, G. (1985). A qualitative study of seatwork in first-grade classrooms. *Elementary School Journal, 86,* 123–140.

Anderson, R. C. (1984). Some reflections on the acquisition of knowledge. *Educational Researcher, 13,* 5–10.

Beck, I. L., & McKeown, M. G. (1988). Toward meaningful accounts in history texts for young learners. *Educational Researcher, 17*, 31–39.

Bereiter, C., & Scardamalia, M. (1985). Cognitive coping strategies and the problem of "inert knowledge." In S. Chipman, J. Segal, & R. Glaser (Eds.), *Thinking and learning skills: Vol. 2. Current research and open questions* (pp. 93–110). Hillsdale, NJ: Lawrence Erlbaum Associates.

Brown, A. L., & Palincsar, A. S. (1989). Guided, cooperative learning and individual knowledge acquisition. In L. Resnick (Ed.), *Knowing and learning: Essays in honor of Robert Glaser* (pp. 393–451). Hillsdale, NJ: Lawrence Erlbaum Associates.

Cole, M. (1985). The zone of proximal development: Where culture and cognition create each other. In J. V. Wertsch (Ed.), *Culture, communication, and cognition: Vygotskian perspectives* (pp. 146–161). Cambridge, UK: Cambridge University Press.

Collins, A., Brown, J. S., & Newman, S. E. (1989). Cognitive apprenticeship: Teaching the craft of reading, writing, and mathematics. In L. B. Resnick (Ed.), *Knowing and learning: Essays in honor of Robert Glaser* (pp. 453–494). Hillsdale, NJ: Lawrence Erlbaum Associates.

Cunningham, P. (1984). What would make workbooks worthwhile? In R. Anderson, J. Osborn, & R. Tierney (Eds.), *Learning to read in American schools: Basal readers and content texts* (pp. 113–120). Hillsdale, NJ: Lawrence Erlbaum Associates.

Durkin, D. (1987). Influences on basal reader programs. *Elementary School Journal, 87*, 331–341.

Englert, C. S., & Raphael, T. E. (1989). Developing successful writers through cognitive strategy instruction. In J. E. Brophy (Ed.), *Advances in research on teaching: Vol. 1. Teaching for meaningful and self-regulated learning* (pp. 105–152). Greenwich, CT: JAI.

Glaser, R. (1984). Education and thinking: The role of knowledge. *American Psychologist, 39*, 93–104.

Hiebert, J., & Lefevre, P. (1986). Conceptual and procedural knowledge in mathematics: An introductory analysis. In J. Hiebert (Ed.), *Conceptual and procedural knowledge: The case of mathematics* (pp. 1–27). Hillsdale, NJ: Lawrence Erlbaum Associates.

Lampert, M. (1986). Knowing, doing, and teaching multiplication. *Cognition and Instruction, 3*, 305–342.

Osborn, J. (1984). The purposes, uses, and contents of workbooks and some guidelines for publishers. In R. Anderson, J. Osborn, & R. Tierney (Eds.), *Learning to read in American schools: Basal readers and content texts* (pp. 45–111). Hillsdale, NJ: Lawrence Erlbaum Associates.

Palincsar, A. S. (1986). The role of dialogue in providing scaffolded instruction. *Educational Psychologist, 21*, 73–98.

Palincsar, A. S., & Brown, A. L. (1984). Reciprocal teaching of comprehension-fostering and comprehension-monitoring activities. *Cognition and Instruction, 1*, 117–175.

Palincsar, A. S., & Brown, A. L. (1989). Classroom dialogues to promote self-regulated comprehension. In J. Brophy (Ed.), *Advances in research on teaching: Vol. 1. Teaching for meaningful understanding and self-regulated learning* (pp. 35–72). Greenwich, CT: JAI.

Perkins, D. N., & Salomon, G. (1989). Are cognitive skills context-bound? *Educational Researcher, 18*, 16–25.

Resnick, L. B. (1987). *Education and learning to think.* Washington, DC: National Academy Press.

Roth, K. J., & Anderson, C. W. (1988). Promoting conceptual change learning from science textbooks. In P. Ramsden (Ed.), *Improving learning: New perspectives* (pp. 109–141). London: Kogan Page Ltd.

Scardamalia, M., & Bereiter, C. (1985). Fostering the development of self-regulation in children's knowledge processing. In S. Chipman, J. Segal, & R. Glaser (Eds.), *Thinking and learning skills: Research and open questions* (Vol. 2, pp. 563–577). Hillsdale, NJ: Lawrence Erlbaum Associates.

Scheu, J., Tanner, D., & Au, K. (1988). Integrating seatwork with the basal lesson. In P. Winograd, K. Wixson, & M. Lipson (Eds.), *Using basal readers to teach reading* (pp. 86–106). New York: Teachers College Press.

Schoenfeld, A. H. (1985). *Mathematical problem solving.* New York: Academic Press.

Tyson-Bernstein, H. (1988). *A conspiracy of good intentions: America's textbook fiasco.* Washington, DC: Council for Basic Education.

Vygotsky, L. S. (1978). *Mind in society: The development of higher psychological processes.* (M. Cole, V. John-Steiner, S. Scribner, & E. Souberman, Eds.). Cambridge, MA: Harvard University Press.

Wertsch, J. (1979). From social interaction to higher psychological processes: A clarification and application of Vygotsky's theory. *Human Development, 22,* 1–22.

── ■ 7 ■──

Ancillary Materials—What's Out There?

Jean Osborn
Karen Decker
University of Illinois at Urbana-Champaign

Commercially developed textbook programs typically contain at least three major components: student textbooks, teachers' manuals, and tests for the assessment of progress. These comprehensive programs also offer a number of ancillary materials, most of which support the major components of a program. Ancillary materials come in a wondrous variety: word cards, big books, picture cards, wall charts, letters to parents, cumulative record cards, word lists, games, sentence boards, picture supplements, flash cards, audio tapes, film strips, workbooks, skill books, blackline masters, map books, lab manuals, software products for teachers and students to use on micro computers, and more.

Some ancillary materials, such as wall charts and picture cards, are developed for teachers to use with students. Some, such as cumulative record cards, are for only the teacher's use. Most ancillary materials, however, are developed for students. Almost all of these materials have the same purpose: to provide students with a medium for practicing, working on, reviewing, or learning independently (often while their teacher is teaching other students) something that is being taught in the classroom.

Ancillary materials are available for almost every school

subject for which there are commercially developed textbook programs. They are available for programs developed to teach the major content areas of science, social studies, and mathematics, as well as the nonmajor content areas—such as health, home economics, consumer education, and foreign languages. They are most available and most numerous, however, in the reading and language arts programs developed for elementary and middle-school classrooms.

In addition to the ancillary materials associated with comprehensive textbook programs, "stand-alone" materials are developed (most often by companies whose main products are workbooks and ditto masters) to supplement instruction in a number of subject areas. These stand-alone materials are not designed to accompany a specific program, but rather are intended to provide activities for students in the program of any publisher. Among the most used of these materials are the alphabet and phonics workbooks developed for kindergarten and first and second grades.

Most ancillary materials, however, are a part of comprehensive programs. And no matter what the subject, the most used of the ancillary materials are workbooks. Workbooks are typically bound in soft covers, containing from 100 to 200 pages. Each of these pages contains a separate task or activity. Workbooks are most often consumable, that is, students write their answers on the pages. Workbooks sometimes have other names: skill builders, skill books, bonus books, and independent practice books. A close relative of workbooks, blackline masters, permit teachers to run off workbook type activities of their choice on school district paper.

In recent years, workbooks have been the focus of attack from many quarters: researchers, who question their value in supporting learning; teachers, who want to have more time for other activities; curriculum planners, who want teachers to be more creative; parents, who accuse schools of giving their children "busy work"; speakers at conventions of reading teachers, who worry about the fragmentation of learning in workbook tasks and propose more wholistic activities; and some college professors, who encourage teachers to develop their own activities. Yet, despite these attacks, workbooks continue to be published and continue to be purchased. In fact, a recent analysis of the kindergarten and first-grade materials of 1989 editions of basal reading programs indicates that these programs contain more work-book pages than previous editions (Durkin, 1989).

What do students *do* when they do workbooks? They fill in blanks, underline words and sentences, and circle words and phrases. They draw lines to match a word to a letter, a word to a word, a picture to a word, and a picture to a picture. They fill in bubbles, and fill in the cells of tables and charts. They select words from lists and write them (or letters that stand for them) in blanks. They select words and sentences in arrays of possible answers to multiple-choice items. They seek and (if they find them) write secret words in blanks. They label diagrams, color in parts of maps, and sometimes, if they can write small enough, write words to identify parts of maps. They do mazes, crossword puzzles, and matrix puzzles. They write sentences ("Give your answers in com-plete sentences") and words ("Write the word on the line") and letters that stand for words or sentences ("Write the letter of the sentence opposite the word it defines").

How can the extensive use of workbooks be explained? Our observation is that well-established educational practices usually stay well established, despite the attacks of their critics, because in some way they serve teachers and students. What does research have to say about the use and effectiveness of workbooks?

RESEARCH ABOUT WORKBOOK USE AND EFFECTIVENESS

Workbooks typically contain exercises one page in length on which students write responses. Classroom observation studies have documented that students spend a great deal of time on the many pages of their workbooks and on the single dittoed pages their teachers have copied from blackline masters. One observer estimated that elementary students complete an average of 1,000 workbook pages a year for reading instruction alone. The most specific information comes from observations of students during classroom periods allocated to reading instruction. One study (Anderson, 1981) found that students spend up to 70% of their instructional time in reading periods doing seatwork—work that frequently consist of "written tasks done without direct teacher supervision." Another study (Anderson, 1984) found that students spent at least 60% of the time allocated for reading instruction on these kinds of activities.

Less information is available about how students spend their allocated time in other subject areas. But, information from publishers of language arts, social studies, and science programs indicates that, although the workbooks of these programs are not as widely used as reading programs, they still account for a significant portion of their sales. And, although the sales of materials do not assure they are actually used, repeat sales of the workbooks of a program are a reasonably strong indication that the workbooks are regularly used in classrooms.

Given the evidence that workbooks are used so extensively in classrooms, what is known about their effect on student learning? Oddly enough, the research about these extensively used materials is not very extensive.

Time-on-task studies shed a little light on how workbook activities affect student achievement. From these studies, we know that students doing independent workbook-type activities (seatwork) typically spend less time-on-task than when working with their teachers in small groups. However, this situation can be affected by the extent to which teachers hold students accountable for seatwork. Students who are held responsible for completing seatwork are more likely to be attentive and stay on task (Fisher et al., 1978). A recent compilation of data from a longitudinal study indicates that the kindergarten and first-grade classrooms in which students spend time in workbooks are typified by higher reading scores (Meyer, Wardrop, & Hastings, 1989).

In a study of eight first-grade classrooms, Anderson (1984) found that from 30% to 60% of the time allocated for students' reading instruction was spent doing some form of seatwork. She observed that some students did not appear to benefit from their seatwork activities:

> There was a group of students whose responses to seatwork frequently were not facilitative to learning . . . they revealed a lack of understanding of the content or skills in the seatwork and they used strategies that were not likely to strengthen their understanding. In general, they did not seem to "make sense" of their seatwork tasks in ways that might further their learning. (p. 93)

Further, investigations by Anderson, Brubaker, Alleman-Brooks, and Duffy (1984), indicate that such students often develop strategies that permit them to simply complete the work on the page, and that these strategies have little or no relationship to learning or even to the content of the page. Anderson et al. contended that the development of such strategies leads to an increase in frustration and additional low achievement.

In several analyses of workbook tasks, Osborn (1984) observed that "a good proportion of workbook tasks are at best imperfect and not very efficient and at worst misleading and confusing" (p. 54). She found that workbook exercises were often irrelevant to what was going on in the rest of the reading lesson, failed to emphasize skills that have an obvious payoff in reading and writing, contained blatant inaccuracies, and presented students with confusing directions.

Her special concern was the use of workbooks with students who have difficulty learning to read. She noted that teachers often turn to supplementary workbooks to provide extra instruction and practice for students in trouble and commented that "Even more pages of irrelevant and pointless tasks may have a particularly adverse effect on children for whom learning to read is difficult" (p. 54).

Workbooks and Publishers

Given this conflicted picture of workbook use and effectiveness, how do publishers view these somewhat controversial materials? We suspect a bit ambiguously. It must be noted that workbooks are not only the most used of the ancillary materials, but for publishers, they are the most profitable of the many components—ancillary and otherwise—of comprehensive programs. Because of the competitive nature of the educational publishing industry, sales figures on the different components of textbook programs are not readily available. We suggest, however, that our assertion can be confirmed by talking to almost any school administrator in charge of textbook purchases or by engaging in a private conversation with a publishing company executive. In fact, an editor of one major basal reading publishing house calculated that his company offers just over 24,000 pages of workbook type materials to accompany its major basal reading program.

The economics of this situation are easily explained. Although hardbound student textbooks are usually the most expensive component of a textbook program, they are typically used and reused in classrooms for about 7 years. Workbooks are much less costly. Because workbooks are "consumable," and must be reordered each year, they account for a large part of the total cost of a reading program. The following example of the per classroom cost of a third-grade basal reading program illustrates why workbooks make a lot of money for their publishers.

Year 1	
Teachers' Manuals	Often free with purchase of other components
Student Textbooks	$12 per pupil × 25 pupils
Workbooks	$3 per pupil × 25 pupils
Total Year 1	$15 per pupil × 25 pupils
Year 2 Workbooks	$3 per pupil
Year 3 Workbooks	$3 per pupil
Year 4 Workbooks	$3 per pupil
Year 5 Workbooks	$3 per pupil
Year 6 Workbooks	$3 per pupil
Year 7 Workbooks	$3 per pupil
Total Year 2 through Year 7	$18 per pupil × 25 pupils

Although the first year cost of the student textbooks and ancillary materials is considerable, the costs of workbooks over 7 years exceeds the per pupil cost of the textbooks and workbooks. For many third-grade classrooms, the amount paid for workbooks is at least double that of the estimate given. Most basal reading programs offer two or more workbooks at each grade level and many classrooms utilize these additional materials. It should also be noted that this estimate includes only the one set of workbooks used for reading instruction and does not include any of the other workbooks that might be used: social studies, mathematics, and some stand-alone materials.

For what subjects do school districts buy most workbooks? Discussions with several major educational publishers confirmed our beliefs: The workbooks associated with the major basal reading programs are the most popular. Following these, in approximate order, are the workbooks that accompany spelling and language arts programs, social studies programs, science programs, and mathematics programs. In addition, the stand-alone sets of workbooks also have a big market, often accounting for a significant part of a school district's workbook purchases.

Workbooks in Other Subjects

Although, as indicated earlier in this chapter, the workbooks of reading programs have been subjected to some research and analysis, the workbooks of social studies and science programs represent a vast unexamined arena. We determined it might be of value to compare the workbooks of reading programs with those of elementary science, social studies, and language arts programs.

To carry out our project, we first acquired the new editions of four basal reading programs, and examined a sometimes, but not always random, sampling of the pages from the fourth-grade workbooks of these programs. We then selected the workbooks of several different social studies, science, and language arts programs. So, in addition to the four reading workbooks, we looked at four social studies workbooks, four science workbooks, and five English language arts workbooks. We also examined the workbooks of the surrounding grade levels of these programs.

As we examined all of these workbooks we considered the types of tasks (e.g., fill-in-the-blanks, match words with pictures, follow a maze), and the content of the tasks (e.g., using short "e," identifying the major rivers of the world, comparing the weight of different substances).

During our examination of these many workbooks, we came to three conclusions. Our first conclusion was that the types of task formats in workbooks were quite numerous and quite variable, but were often common across subject matter and across grade levels. The second conclusion was that the content of the workbooks was for the most part related to the content of the programs, but often in a cursory and superficial manner. Our third conclusion involved students: To be successful at doing workbook tasks, students must be able to understand, manipulate, and handle large numbers of workbook formats, in addition to being very well acquainted with the workbook's content. We discuss these conclusions in the next section.

Types of Workbook Formats.   We were impressed with the variety of the types of workbook formats with which students have to cope to perform well on workbook pages. Often each succeeding page presents a different format. For example, in one 182-page workbook, we found 23 major and distinct formats; in an 80-page social studies workbook, we found 18 formats; and, in a 92-page science workbook, we found 21 formats. Most formats have variations; occasionally, more than one format appears on a single page.

We were not only impressed with the number of formats that students encounter in any given workbook, but we were also impressed by the number of formats that were common to most of the grade levels of the same program, as well as to the workbooks of all the subjects and all the publishers we examined. For example, the multiple choice format were found in the grade levels within each subject area, and also across the subject areas—from reading, to social studies, to science, and to language arts. When students learn how to successfully choose the right answer from a variety of choices, they acquire a skill that they will use in all grade levels, in all subjects, and probably in the tests that they will take for the rest of their lives.

We categorized the most common format types. These appear in Tables 7.1 and 7.2.

The subject of each program appears at the top of each column; the letter represents the publisher code (e.g., Reading B and English B are from the same publisher). Table 7.1 includes three major categories of format types; these are listed to the left: *Puzzles, Visuals,* and *Facsimilies.* The most common specific format types are listed under each category label. A letter "x" in a right-hand column indicates multiple appearances of a format type in a workbook. In sorting formats, it was often difficult to put one style of working through a task exclusively in one format type. Many pages were "blends" of several formats, and variations on several different types. Nonetheless, a number of formats stood out as common; these are now described:

Puzzles.   This format type includes a variety of puzzle activities: crossword puzzles, the making and breaking of codes, unscrambling letters, searching for secret words

TABLE 7.1

Format Types and Ways of Responding

	Reading A	Reading B	Reading C	Reading D	Social Studies A	Social Studies B	Social Studies C	Social Studies D	English A	English B	Spelling A	Spelling B	Science A (Lab book)	Science B	Science C	Health A	Language Arts A
Puzzles																	
Crossword		X				X	X	X	X	X	X	X		X	X	X	X
Lettergrid						X	X	X			X	X		X	X	X	X
Secret word					X	X	X	X			X	X		X	X	X	X
Code/scrambled			X			X						X	X	X	X	X	X
Visuals																	
Graphs	X	X	X	X		X	X		X	X	X			X	X	X	X
Maps	X	X	X	X	X	X	X				X		X	X	X	X	X
Charts	X	X	X	X	X	X	X	X		X	X	X	X	X	X	X	X
Diagram labeling	X	X	X	X	X	X	X	X	X	X	X		X	X	X	X	X
Facsimilies																	
Dictionary	X	X	X	X					X	X	X						
Index	X	X	X	X				X									
Newspaper	X	X	X	X		X											X
Reference	X	X	X	X					X		X						
Letters	X	X		X					X								X
Table of contents	X	X							X		X						
TV guide	X	X									X	X					

169

TABLE 7.2
Ways of Responding

	Reading A	Reading B	Reading C	Reading D	Social Studies A	Social Studies B	Social Studies C	Social Studies D	English A	English B	Spelling A	Spelling B	Science A (Lab book)	Science B	Science C	Health A	Language Arts A
Response Types																	
Elimination	X	X	X		X	X	X	X	X	X	X	X	X	X	X	X	X
Underlining	X	X			X	X	X	X	X	X	X	X				X	
Matching		X	X	X	X	X		X	X	X	X	X		X	X		
Multiple choice	X	X	X	X	X	X	X	X	X	X	X			X	X		
Fill in blanks	X	X	X	X	X	X	X	X	X	X				X	X	X	
Writing						X	X	X	X	X			X	X	X	X	X
Ordering	X	X	X		X				X	X			X			X	
Read and Respond																	
Short passages		X	X	X	X	X	X	X	X	X	X	X	X			X	X
Directions																	
Location																	
Confusing	X	X					X	X					X				
Multiple Directions	X		X	X	X	X	X	X	X	X	X	X					X

170

in answers or pictures, and letter grids (a square of letters that contain words that are to be circled).

Visuals. This format type includes map work, diagram labeling, picture recognition, and completing charts or graphs.

Facsimilies. This format type includes reprints from a portion of a book (e.g., dictionary pages, portions of an index, tables of contents, pages from a television guide), illustrations of a shelf of alphabetized encyclopedias, reproductions of cards from a card catalog, and newspaper articles.

Our examination of format types led us to categorize some formats by the responses they required. The most frequent ways students must respond to the directions on workbook pages are summarized in Table 7.2.

Again, the subject of each program appears at the top of each column. The ways of responding are listed on the left. We have divided these into three rather uneven categories. The first, *Response Types,* contains a number of the common responses required for the completion of workbook tasks; the second, *Read and Respond,* identifies a format type common to essentially all workbooks; and the third, *Directions,* identifies two types of possibly confusing directions. The following is a brief description of each of the entries:

Response Types. Elimination (in which the number of answers listed equals the number of blanks to be filled in); underlining (a word, a phrase, or a sentence); matching (copying or drawing lines from letters to words or a part of a picture to a whole picture); multiple choice (in a variety of forms); fill in the blank (with a word—with the possible answers sometimes provided and sometimes not); written (a phrase, sentence, or paragraph in often not very adequate space); ordering (in which the events of a paragraph or a story are to be arranged in sequence).

Read and Respond. Portions of text, usually one to three paragraphs that tell a story or present information. Questions about the text follow.

Directions. Two potential problems in directions: location of directions and multiple directions. *Multiple directions* indicates a format in which students are asked to do two or more activities to complete the task; they may be asked to circle a phrase and then write a word, or to underline a portion of a sentence and then fill in a blank. Sometimes a task requires the students to go through several embedded steps to complete the page.

As the tables reveal, most ways of responding (and variations) were found in all the workbooks we examined—reading, social studies, science, and language arts.

Success at Working in Workbooks

What do students who breeze through workbook tasks know? We hypothesized that to be successful in workbook activities, students have to not only be comfortable with the content of workbook tasks, but they also have to become format experts. We suspect that when such students begin to work in their assigned workbook pages, they either recognize quickly the response demands of a format and set to work, or understand very well how to figure out the meaning of often unclear and ambiguous directions.

An examination of the workbook pages that are typically assigned for one day in a subject reveals that students will encounter five or more different formats. For example, in one day's assignment in a reading program, a student must work through five formats that are contained in three workbook pages and deal with five sets of directions. These directions are as follows:

On the first page:
   A. Match each word with its definition. Write the letter of the definition on the line to the left of the definition.
   B. Below are some parts of sentences about the story. Match the beginning with the end of each sentence. Write the letter of the end of each sentence on the blank.
On the second page:
   A. A contraction combines two words. An apostrophe takes the place of the missing letters. Draw a line under the contraction that is formed by combining the two words on the left.
        and

B. Complete each sentence. Write the contraction that is formed by combining the two words.

On the third page:

These directions are for hiking from Emerald Lake to the base of Thunder Mountain.

1. Start at Emerald Lake.
2. Walk down Pine Trail.
3. Walk left on Bear Trail.
4. Walk right on Deer Trail.
5. Walk right on Lichen Trail.
6. Arrive at Thunder Mountain.

Use the map to write these six directions for hiking from Emerald Lake to the base of Thunder Mountain.

We reasoned that children who can independently shift from task to task are very flexible and able to adapt easily to different numerous formats and sets of directions. We decided to give such children a label: *workbookers.*

Workbookers are good at recognizing and figuring out how to do different formats. Given the similarity of format types across subjects, we concluded that such skill serves them well in the workbook activities of any program—whether it be social studies, spelling, English, handwriting, or science. As we examined the variations among format types, we came to realize, however, that the skill of workbookers includes, not only the ability to cope with a number of different format types, but also involves the capacity to deal with an enormous amount of slight variation among similar, but not exactly the same, formats. For example: In responding to the multiple-choice format, sometimes students must fill out the correct answer in a bubble; other times, they must underline it, circle it, or write it out. (And furthermore, the letters they circle might reveal a secret word or phrase.) We suggest that students who perform well on these variations (the workbookers) have learned a great deal about both generalization and discrimination, and about how to differentiate and relate their responses to the context of a given format or a certain subject. And that specifically, they have three sets of workbook behaviors well in hand: (a) recognizing and attending to the demands of different formats, (b) adapting to the variations of formats, and (c) proficiency in response modes.

Something Else

As we analyzed the formats, the response forms, and the content of the workbooks, we gradually became aware of something else common to many workbook tasks. It also occurred to us that workbookers understand this "something else" very well. For us to define this something else requires us to step back and formulate a couple of common-sense assumptions about the goals of workbooks.

We assume that workbooks are developed to provide students with practice in learning how to do something, or to provide them with help in remembering something. We also assume (and highly recommend) that workbooks be correlated closely with the rest of what the students are learning about a subject. For example, if a teacher-directed lesson in reading is about finding the main ideas of an article in the textbook, an associated workbook task would require the students to find main ideas in passages appearing in the workbook, as well as in what they read in their textbook. Or, if a social studies lesson is how to determine directions on maps, a companion workbook page would have students do map work by following directions.

A reasonable belief that emerges from these two assumptions is that the content of a workbook should resemble the fundamental characteristics of the program it accompanies. In which case, reading workbook tasks should contain content that is like the text of a book (or a specific aspect of reading instruction); science workbook tasks should contain content that is like learning about science (or applying scientific information to a particular problem).

As we examined workbooks across subjects, however, we came to realize that, quite often, the content of workbook pages did not resemble the fundamental characteristics of the subject of the program. For example, one of the goals of reading instruction is that students learn to read connected text. As they do so, they must understand that what is communicated in one sentence in a paragraph is usually related in some way to the preceding or subsequent sentence.

Yet in workbooks, lists of sentences in some tasks that look disconnected are to be read as connected text. For example, in one very common type of fill-in-the blank task, the numbered sentences must be read as connected text:

1. After the three bears left their _____, they walked through the _____.
2. When they returned _____, they knew something was _____.

Whereas in an equally common type of task, the list of sentences must be read as disconnected text. For example,

1. Robert divided the melon into two _____.
2. Tony used the _____ to find the coal mine.
3. Her handwriting is _____ than yours.

Children doing this task are going to be in trouble if they try to find a referent in Sentence 1 for the pronoun in Sentence 2. The trouble will be caused by applying what they know about reading connected text in a book to reading this workbook text. On the contrary, they must suspend what they know about reading connected text to perform this task.

Another example: Research about story grammar and story structure has had a lot of appeal to many teachers, and as a matter of fact, to many publishers. The idea is that stories have an identifiable structure, and that to better understand and remember them, students can learn to identify and label the elements of stories. In many basal reading programs, the instructions to the teacher and specified questions in the teacher's manual reflect these notions. Yet, the pages of reading workbooks contain lots of paragraphs labeled as *stories* that wouldn't make it through a story grammarian's structure. Equally distressing is that a lot of expository passages are labeled as stories, for example, "Read the following story about how animals use their teeth."

As we thought about the differences between fundamental characteristics of subjects and their manifestations in workbooks, we gradually came to the conclusion that the something else that successful workbookers understand is how to adjust (or perhaps to even suspend belief in), what they know from elsewhere to accommodate to the task demands of workbooks. In attempting to analyze the components of this something else, we concluded the existence of a "workbook genre" that consists of a complex set of conventions unique to the task found in workbooks. We believe that this genre has evolved, not intentionally, but rather through the years and years of labor that workbook writers have devoted to the creation of workbook tasks. Although this genre has never been considered by literary experts, we think it has as many nuances as a short story; furthermore, it can be as confusing in form and style as some contemporary poetry.

Should the workbook genre be taught? The rationale for instructional practice in a variety of genres has a basis in research about reading. It has been shown that readers employ different cognitive processes when they read, for example, narrative text as compared to expository text, and that instruction can help them understand and use these processes. Although there exists some research about direction following, to our knowledge, the processes associated with how students deal with the content of workbooks, while simultaneously following varying formats, has not been seriously studied. We suggest, however, that an examination of the workbook behaviors of workbookers would reveal some very specific cognitive—and metacognitive—strategies. We also believe that such an examination would reveal some specific characteristics of the workbook genre. We anticipate that it would be easy to label some of these characteristics as desirable, and some as undesirable.

We do not want to promote the existence of the workbook genre without asking a couple of important questions: What can we learn about the task demands of this genre from the analyses of workbook pages? And what kind of advice can we offer publishers that will permit them to (a) write workbooks so as to make this genre less illusive for all of those students who must deal with it, and (b) provide help for students who do not—and probably without help will not learn about it. In our attempt to formulate this advice, we reexamined some workbook tasks to predict their effects on the students working through them. We found we could divide these effects into two groups: *intended effects,* and *unintended effects.* We discuss our views of both the intended and unintended effects of workbook tasks in the following section.

Intended and Unintended Effects of Workbook Tasks

We first discuss the intended effects of workbook tasks for teachers and for students. Workbooks can serve teachers in two fundamental ways: management and evaluation. These aspects of workbook use are discussed here.

Management. Many teachers use workbook activities to help manage their classroom time and (as everyone knows), workbooks keep some students busy while their teacher works with other groups of students. As is evident, workbooks provide teachers with prepared practice materials to accompany the instruction contained in the reading and other subject area programs they are using.

Evaluating Student Performance. Something that is less evident should also be pointed out: Completed workbook tasks provide teachers with some very specific information about student performance. In day-to-day classroom activities, such information is not always so readily available. For example, a teacher working with a group of students during a reading period asks one student to read a passage or to answer some questions. If that student's response is acceptable, the teacher calls on another student. The teacher must assume that the students who are not responding are able to read the passage and answer the questions. With workbook activities, no one is passed over and no student can "sit silently" while others are answering. Of course it must be noted that workbook pages can be used to evaluate student progress with confidence only if the activities reflect important aspects of the instructional program.

Workbooks can also serve students. For example, workbook activities can provide the following:

Practice. Many concepts and skills require practice. Workbooks can provide that practice, and they can do it differentially, that is, with extra attention to those aspects of learning that are more difficult.

Writing. By requiring that students write words, sentences, and paragraphs, workbooks can provide practice

in writing. Such tasks can be, in a sense, a bridge
between "pure reading" and "pure writing."

Independent Practice.   Workbooks give students practice
in working independently—a component of learning, the
importance of which stretches far beyond doing workbook tasks.

Review and Synthesis.   Workloads can provide review of
what is taught and activities in which students must
synthesize what they have learned and make applications to new situations.

Sense of Accomplishment.   Workbooks can provide students with a sense of accomplishment, especially when
the work is worthwhile, challenging but "do-able," and
has an occasional reward.

Direction Following and Test Taking.   Workbooks and
experiences with a variety of test-taking formats provide
students with practice in following directions.

Do the effects of workbook tasks on students always have
the intended effects? We suspect not, and believe that some
of the research discussed earlier in this chapter supports this
suspicion, as confirmed by talking with teachers who work
with children having difficulty with workbooks. It is with
these children in mind—the nonworkbookers—that we began
to worry about the potential of workbook tasks for unintended effects.

Our conviction is that students who understand the workbook genre (workbookers) are more or less immune to the
unintended effects of workbooks, but that it is the other less
knowledgeable students who suffer from their unintended
effects. Furthermore, the consequences of the unintended
effects of workbook performance on students can easily
extend to their achievement in other, more central, aspects of
their school performance. Osborn recalls observing a group of
children in a fourth-grade classroom who read very well (at
grade level), but who had a great deal of trouble with the
details of reading contained in their workbook tasks. For
example, in one task, these students had to determine
whether the ending *ed* at the end of words on a very long list
made the *ed* or the *et* sound. The daily poor grades on this
kind of activity contained a very negative, and in this case,

unwarranted message, about the students' general reading performance.

The unintended effects of workbook tasks are difficult to categorize. In an attempt to do so, we combined memories of our classroom observations of children working in workbooks with our own analyses of workbook tasks to produce a list, with examples, of some of the possible unintended effects of workbooks. In no way is this list complete, nor has it been verified by careful research. We propose it as a caution to teachers and submit it as a modest proposal to publishers.

• Success goes to those who already know the answers.

Obviously, some concepts are not suitable to workbook tasks. In many tasks, the amount of prior knowledge a student possesses would seem to have a critical influence on performance. For example, a workbook task with pictures of lampshades, curtains, windows, eyeglasses, glasses of water, and furniture illustrating the concepts *transparent, translucent,* and *opaque* could possibly serve as a review for students already acquainted with these concepts. For students not acquainted with either these concepts or this vocabulary, such a picture task does not promise much enlightenment and therefore not much success.

• Language is not always what it seems to be.

Many workbook tasks require students to have a firm understanding of such relative terms as *many* and *few,* and of how negation usually works in cause and effect statements. And sometimes they have to put aside their own knowledge. For example, a task that requires students to determine whether *many people* or *few people* live in deserts because *there is not enough water for their needs* or *the climate is comfortable* will be resolved easily by the student who knows that *few people* must go along with a statement containing *not.* If this student lives in Las Vegas, a desert location with lots of people who presumably use lots of water everyday, she will have to be a real workbooker to come up with the "right" answer.

- Language is harder that it should be.

To tell what happened first and what happened next is usually pretty easy for students—workbookers and nonworkbookers alike. They have little trouble remembering and accurately describing the order of events in real life and in discussing the order of events in narratives. The sequence of events is a favorite topic of the workbook task. The following example is an adaptation of one task:

In each sentence, underline the event that happens first.

1. We came to the door after we walked through the dark hall.
2. To unlock the door we had to search for the key.
3. Before we could climb down the ladder into the dark basement we had to search for the light switch.
4. We saw the cans and buckets floating in the water after we smelled the damp, humid air.

Many students make a lot of mistakes in tasks like these. Why? We suggest that the language of these sentences is not the straightforward language of children who are telling about "What happened." Rather, the task is an exercise is the actual and implied use of *before* and *after,* words that do not ordinarily occur in such density. Thus, for some students, this kind of task makes language harder than it is and harder than it should be.

- Directions are not worth reading.

Teachers often complain that their students don't read directions. Because of their workbook expertise, workbookers probably save a lot of time by not reading most directions— on the other hand, they know when and how to seek some help when they need it, either by reading the directions, consulting with a friend, or talking to their teacher. Well-written directions would probably be of help to students who are not natural workbookers. But, they would have to have had some good experiences reading and following "followable" directions. The following directions are from some much used workbooks. They have been only faintly altered.

We think they are confusing enough to cause most students—workbookers and nonworkbookers alike—to stop reading directions.

> In Part A, choose the beginning that makes that part of the sentence correct. Draw a line around the correct words that are in parentheses. Then make a line from the beginning of each sentence in Part A to a reason in Part B.

> Write the letter of each description at right in the blank in front of the number of the correct geographical feature.

> Use the context of the story to help you figure out the meanings of the underlined words in the following story. The underlined words in the story are listed below with three lettered meanings. Circle the letter of the correct meaning.

> Write the number of the word on the part of the illustration that the word describes. Read pages 42–51 in your book if you need help. Some words may be used more than once. At the bottom of the page, write sentences that include the words not used in the picture.

> The column on the left below contains some words that appeared in pages 35–45 of the textbook. The definitions of these words appear in the right-hand column. In the space before each word in the left-hand column, write the number of its correct definition that you read in the right-hand column. Then look below and search for the same words in the word-search puzzle.

• Meaning and description are just letters or numbers.

Tasks in which numbers and letters stand for something else are common in workbooks. Even the most diligent of workbookers will have trouble checking their work when their completed pages read, for example:

D 1. jury
H 2. congress
I 3. president
B 4. supreme court

The letters in this kind of task stand for definitions that appear elsewhere on the page. In another example, numbers that are to be written on an illustration representing vocabulary words that are listed above the picture. In still another task, students are to match the letters on a picture of a piece of laboratory equipment in the blanks next to descriptions below the picture:

1. Heating is applied here. <u>D</u>
2. Cooling is applied here. <u>H</u>
3. Where water is changed into steam. <u>J</u>
4. Where steam is changed into water. <u>R</u>

We think that "Heating is applied here. <u>D</u>" is not very informative.

• In addition to ending up as letters and numbers, descriptions and definitions almost always come out even.

That there are as many blanks and terms as there are descriptive phrases and definitions means that students focus on an elimination game, rather than on meaning—especially when working with the last few items on a page. That there are as many "answers" as blanks to fill in assures that the students never read the final item. By the simple move of providing more possible answers than blanks to fill in, workbook developers would require the students to think about, and select from a greater pool of possibilities.

• You have to be very smart to figure out secrets.

Sometimes workbook tasks involve a filling in the blanks to determine a "secret word" at the bottom of the page. In this type of task, students are to indicate, for example, if statements are true or false by circling letters under columns marked True and False:

	True	False
1. Tennessee is famous for its chicken ranches.	E	O
2. The Appalachian Highlands are in three states.	M	A
3. Mt. Whitney is the tallest mountain in California.	F	G
4. The Cumberland Gap is located in Florida.	T	I
5. Winters are long in Alaska.	S	B

After completing 17 items by circling the letters under the true and false columns, the students are in a position to try to figure out the secret word at the end of the page. The workbookers will probably figure out this word after they get a few of its letters in place. In fact, given the memory demands of this kind of task, they may use the letters of the secret word to help them with any items they are having trouble with. Only if they have everything right above is it likely that other students will have a chance of finding the identity of the secret word. If they bother to worry about what the letter S has to do with Tennessee and the letter O has to do with the Appalachian Highlands they are in real trouble.

• The best way to use context is to leave it.

A number of workbook tasks are set up so that students read a two or three paragraph "story" containing some underlined words. They are then to complete a set of items that require them to identify correct synonyms or definitions for the underlined words. Workbookers often ignore the "story" and go straight to the items. On the other hand, students who would benefit from reading the words in the context of the text and then checking out their meanings often go straight to the items—probably because they find the process of reading a sentence in the story, and then skipping down to an item to be too distracting and time-consuming to be helpful.

• Life may not be a game, but it sure is a puzzle.

Puzzle formats are common to workbooks. Students work with scrambled words, crossword puzzles, words hidden in boxes, and words hidden in arrays of seemingly random letters. How such activities affect learning is not a topic of any research that we know about. We suggest, however, that given the number of puzzles that appear in workbooks, that it is worthy of some investigation.

   We recently received a newsletter with the following puzzle about heart disease. After we read the directions for this puzzle we decided that maybe workbooks do prepare people for adult life, and that knowing how to figure out unclear directions is a skill that serves one in real life. Please notice that the last sentence asks us to find the words in the puzzle *below*. That the puzzle is *to the side* of the page caused us— old workbookers that we are—no trouble at all.

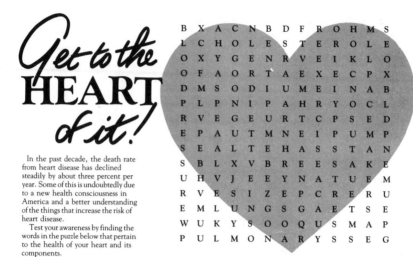

In the past decade, the death rate from heart disease has declined steadily by about three percent per year. Some of this is undoubtedly due to a new health consciousness in America and a better understanding of the things that increase the risk of heart disease.

Test your awareness by finding the words in the puzzle below that pertain to the health of your heart and its components.

FIG. 7.1   Reprinted by permission of Health Alliance Medical Plans, Inc.

CONCLUSION

In our examination of the workbook "scene," we do not conclude that workbooks should be eliminated from American classrooms. We do not join those who would get rid of workbooks, no matter what. On the contrary, we are concerned about the reality of the need (by teachers and students) for the intended effects of these materials. So, the question is, can workbooks be improved so that more reliably, their effects are as intended. We believe that they can. The first challenge to the publishers who create them and to the teachers who buy them is a careful examination of their effects—both intended and unintended—on the students who use them. The next challenge is to figure out how to produce workbook tasks that are both "do-able" and worthwhile. We believe that the workbook genre should not be mysterious, and furthermore, we believe that every child can become a workbooker.

ACKNOWLEDGMENT

The work on which this publication was based was supported in part by the Office of Educational Research and Improvement under

Cooperative Agreement No. G 0087-C1001–90. It is a deliverable for Study 2.2.1.6(c), as specified in the Cooperative Agreement. This publication does not necessarily reflect the views of the agency supporting the research.

REFERENCES

Durkin, D. (1989). *New kindergarten basal reader materials: What's a teacher supposed to do with all this?* (Tech. Rep. No. 475). Urbana-Champaign: University of Illinois, Center for the Study of Reading.

Anderson, L. (1981). *Student responses to seatwork: Implications for the study of students' cognitive processing* (Research Series No. 102). East Lansing: Michigan State University, The Institute for Research on Teaching.

Anderson, L. (1984). The environment of instruction: The function of seatwork in a commercially developed curriculum. In G. G. Duffy, L. R. Roehler, & J. Mason (Eds.), *Comprehension instruction: Perspectives and suggestions* (pp. 93–6). New York: Longman.

Fisher, C., Berliner, D., Filby, N., Marliave, R., Cohen, L., Dishaw, M., & Moore, J. (1978). *Teaching and learning in elementary schools: A summary of the beginning teacher evaluation study.* San Francisco, CA: Far West Laboratory for Educational Research and Development.

Meyer, L. A., Wardrop, J. L., & Hastings, C. N. (1989). *Interim report of trends from a longitudinal study of the development of reading comprehension ability.* Urbana-Champaign: University of Illinois, Center for the Study of Reading.

Anderson, L., Brubaker, N. L., Alleman-Brooks, J., & Duffy, G. G. (1984). *Making seatwork work.* (Research Series No. 142). East Lansing: Michigan State University, The Institute for Research on Teaching.

Osborn, J. (1984). The purposes, uses and contents of workbooks and some guidelines for publishers. In R. C. Anderson, J. Osborn, & R. J. Tierney (Eds.), *Learning to read in American schools: Basal readers and content texts* (pp. 40–55). Hillsdale, NJ: Lawrence Erlbaum Associates.

Author Index

A

Abel, R. R., 99, 105, *111*
Alleman-Brooks, J., 142, *158*, 165, *185*
Allington, R. L., 47, 48, 52, 60, *65*, 67
Alvermann, D. E., 62, *65*
Anderson, C. W., 140, 145, 146, *158*, *160*
Anderson, J. R., 3, 4, *45*
Anderson, L., 163, 164, 165, *185*
Anderson, L. M., 142, *158*
Anderson, R. C., 4, *42*, 138, *158*
Anderson, T. H., 49, *65*, 86, *93*
Andre, T., 49, 56, 57, 59, *65*, 83, *93*
Anglin, G. J., 95, 97, 106, *112*, 128, *133*
Applebee, A. N., 59, *65*
Armbruster, B. B., 49, *65*, 86, *93*
Au, K., 54, *65*, 143, *160*

B

Baillet, S. D., 4, *44*
Baird, W., 3, *44*
Barrett, T. C., 72, 74, *93*, *94*
Bartlett, S., 8, *43*
Baumann, J. F., 3, *41*
Beck, I. L., 3, *41*, 92, *93*, 140, *159*
Begley, S., 100, *111*
Bereiter, C., 64, *66*, 149, *159*, *160*
Berliner, D., 55, 57, *66*, 164, *185*
Berry, J. K., 105, 107, *112*
Berry, S. L., 9, *44*
Bloom, B. S., 71, 74, *93*
Bluth, G. J., 4, *45*
Bond, S. J., 3, *46*
Brandt, D. M., 4, *41*, *45*
Bransford, J. D., 8, *41*, 103, *111*
Branthwaite, A., 8, *43*
Brennan, A. D., 3, *41*
Bridge, C. A., 3, *41*
Britton, B. K., 3, 4, 6, 9, 10, 18, 20, 32, 36, *41*, *42*
Bromage, B. K., 100, 105, *111*
Brooks, L., 7, *44*
Brooks, L. W., 7, *42*
Brown, A. L., 63, *67*, 143, 153, *159*
Brown, J. S., 149, *159*
Brown, P., 4, *44*
Brubaker, N., 142, *158*, 165, *185*
Bruning, R. H., 49, *65*, 86, *93*

187

Subject Index

A

Adding elements to texts, 3, 7, 8
  adding linguistic elements, 7
  adding paralinguistic elements
    advanced organizers, 36
    headings, 7, 21, 36, 39
    logical connectives, 7
    preview sentences, 7
    signaling, 7
    summaries, 7, 36
    typographical cues, 7, 21, 36
    typographical emphasizers, 7
    underlining, 7
Adult learners, 2, 7
Aircraft mechanics, 7
Analogies, 100, 102
Ancillary materials, 161
Army job tracks, 2, 3
Artificially constructed texts, 4, 8
Audio tapes, 161
  big books, 161
  filmstrips, 161
  flash cards, 161
  games, 161
  letters to parents, 161
  map books, 161

  picture cards, 161
  sentence boards, 161
  skill books, 161
  software products, 161
  wall charts, 161
  word cards, 161
  workbooks, 161
Authors, 37–39
Auxiliary materials, 135–157
  design and use of, 149–157
  in reading instruction, 141–145
  in science instruction, 145–149
  multiple representation of
    ideas, 152–153
  scaffolding students' thinking,
    149–152
  social contexts for performance,
    153–154
  supporting teachers' use of,
    157–158

B

Basal readers, 50–53
Basal reading program, 165
Biology, 2, 7